Simply British

Matthew Greener
Francis Kisby
David Lynch
Ben Meekings
Alan Sewell

Storyman Publishing

ISBN 0-9543134-2-9

Published in Great Britain in 2002 by
Storyman Publishing
Swallowfield, Exeter Hill, Tiverton, Devon EX16 4PL

Copyright © Text Matthew Greener, Francis Kisby, David Lynch,
       Ben Meekings and Alan Sewell 2002

All rights reserved

This book is sold subject to the condition that it shall not, by way of trade or otherwise, be resold, hired out, or otherwise circulated without the publisher's prior consent in any form or binding or cover other than that in which it is published and without a similar condition, including this condition, being imposed on the subsequent purchaser. No part of this publication may be reproduced, stored in a retrieval system, or transmitted in any form or by any means, electronic, mechanical, photocopying, recording, or otherwise, without the publisher's permission.

Printed in Great Britain by Short Run Press Ltd, Exeter

Contents

Introduction 1
The History of Cheesemaking 3
The Cheesemaking Process 6
So Many Cheeses … 12
What to Look For: Determining a Good Cheese 15
Storing the Cheese 19
Making a Great Cheeseboard 23
Cutting and Slicing Cheese 29
Cheese and … Drinks 33
32 Things You Never Knew You Wanted To Know About Cheese 36
The Cheeses 40
Appleby's Cheshire 41
Beenleigh Blue 44
Berkswell 47
Bishop Kennedy 50
Cashel Blue 53
Celtic Promise 56
Cheddar 59
Colston Bassett Stilton 63
Cornish Brie 67
Cornish Yarg 70
Derby 73
Devon Blue 76
Ducketts Caerphilly 79
Duddleswell 82
Durrus 84
Gubbeen Smoked 88
Hereford Hop 91
Lanark Blue 94
Lancashire 97
Leicester 101
Milleens 104

Olde Gloster	108
Sharphams	111
Swaledale	114
Ticklemore	117
Tymsboro	120
Waterloo	123
Shepherd's Purse Wensleydale	126
Wigmore	129
Yorkshire Blue	132
Basing	135
Bosworth	136
Buxton Blue	137
Capricorn Goats	138
Chabis Sussex	139
Cooleney	140
Croghan	141
Harbourne Blue	142
Leafield	143
Pentlands	144
Ribblesdale	145
Vulscombe	146
Yorkshire Feta	147
Don't Worry!	148
Glossary	150
Useful Websites	160
Acknowledgements	161
Photographs	162

Foreword

This book has been a pleasure to produce. Many thanks to all the people who have helped us develop this into what we feel is a comprehensive, yet interesting, guide to the best of British Cheese.

We hope you enjoy reading this as much as we enjoyed creating it.

Introduction

'To Encourage and Inspire'

This is precisely what we aim to do! How do you tell if a cheese is ripe? What would you ideally serve with Caerphilly? Should you store cheese in cling film? And how can you present it as a final flourish to a dinner party in an appealing and eye-catching manner?

Answers to these questions and more form the basis of this book. Within these pages we hope to bring to light the story of cheese in all its mystery-shrouded glory. If you're one of the people – like us – who have been intrigued by this versatile and wonderful product but been too afraid to ask, this is the book for you. Our aim in writing this has been to strip away all the complexity and formality that seems to come with the topic and take a light-hearted yet informative approach instead.

After all, why should this subject provoke such fear in us? What justification can there possibly be for hiding it away and reserving it only for those deemed knowledgeable enough to serve it? This we cannot answer – however, in writing the following book we hope to prove that cheese should not be viewed in such a terrifying light and can be enjoyed by anyone with an interest in it.

And there's more. This book focuses on cheeses produced solely in the UK. The reason behind this is to try and demonstrate to you that it is not simply France and Italy that deserve all the recognition for producing fine cheeses. It's about time the UK was put on the map for doing so too. Having read this and tasted some of our recommendations for yourself, we hope you'll agree!

So have a read. Leaf through the following chapters and delve into a subject we found more and more fascinating as the story progressed. Cast off those doubts and fears and find out what it's all about – but above all, have fun in doing so.

The authors

> *"It is refreshing to see a group of young people interested in such a subject. Hopefully this book will go some way to increasing people's opinion of and confidence in British Cheese"*

Randolph Hodgson (2002).

The History of Cheesemaking

Cheesemaking has been recorded as far back as 6000BC, but we can safely say that people knew about cheesemaking before they knew how to write, and hence the lack of information before this date! There are many theories as to how cheese was first discovered. Here is one of them:

A long time ago in the Middle East a wandering nomad was lucky enough to stumble across a goat. Walking long distances at a time was thirsty work and this goat provided him with much needed refreshment; he milked it for all he could! Not having the luxury of a thermos flask the nomad stored the milk in his hand-made skin bag and set off early in the morning. Little did he know that whilst he was carrying the bag the sugars in the milk and the heat from the hot sun had caused fermentation and the splitting of the milk into curds and whey. At noon the nomad decided to take a rest and upon opening his bag was shocked with what he saw! Being an adventurous guy (so his wife said) and in desperate need of refreshment, he decided to eat the curds and drink the whey! The rest, shall we say, is history!

Not quite …

After that amazing discovery by the wandering nomad, word got around and cultures and civilisations throughout the globe began to develop and refine their own methods of making cheese. Many are still being used today and are remain individual to that region.

One such civilisation that revolutionised cheesemaking was the Romans, who were responsible for contributing to the development of Feta and Parmesan – two very popular cheeses today. As the Roman Empire grew, so did their expertise; they introduced herbs, spices and even smoking to the cheese, continually developing the process. When their empire eventually collapsed the cheesemaking process continued to spread and evolve throughout Europe, each region creating its own style. The Swiss, for example, used their mountainous land to produce the Emmental cheese, whereas in the fertile lowlands of the Netherlands, where farming was developing at a fast pace, Edam and Gouda were being produced. Production regions were found to have their own characteristics, which were then often reflected in the cheese. This is one of the reasons why certain cheeses are only produced successfully in particular areas.

Cheesemaking was a local farm industry until the 19th century; when in 1851 the first cheese factory was built in New York. Demand for the product was growing – people loved it! By 1845 a group of Swiss immigrants had moved to America and used their expertise to make foreign cheeses. The industry was developing quickly and many factories began to open, each making different varieties. By the late 1800's only a small proportion of cheeses were made in the traditional farmhouse style as factory production took over providing the product to the masses. The demand for cheese continued to grow, and with it grew the factories, which was the only way to keep up with the huge demand.

From this initial serendipitous discovery to a now highly refined process, cheesemaking has developed throughout the years into a multi-million pound industry which is still continuing to grow.

There is, however, more to today's cheese than the bulk-produced varieties found on supermarket shelves. Though somewhat fewer in number than in past years, traditionally made varieties from smaller, specialised outlets continue to be produced and enjoyed by a multitude of people. It is these cheeses that are the subject of this book.

The Cheesemaking Process

A Quick Note

Before we look at this subject in more detail, we should probably point out a couple of issues regarding the making of cheese and their implications.

Firstly, we consider it important to mention that many of the modern methods used in the bulk manufacture of cheese have detracted from its reputation of being an 'art combined with a science', as many people believe it to be. Artificial colours and flavourings combined with highly technical processing techniques have all resulted in the sterile, synthetic cheese we have become accustomed to buying in supermarkets. Though this is obviously not true of every type found on the store shelves, we believe it is this 'fake' cheese that is largely to blame for so many people having misconceptions about its appeal.

The real beauty of cheese – and this is partly what inspired us to write this book – lies in those produced by smaller, more specialised outlets by individuals with a real love for the product. Often hidden away in the middle of nowhere, small farmhouse-style outlets produce lesser quantities, but infinitely superior cheeses that, globally, remain largely and lamentably unknown.

The truth, as any connoisseur will tell you, is that the UK has as much to offer as any of the other, better-known cheese producing nations such as France and Italy. Cheese varieties from within our shores stretch far beyond the household names of Cheddar and Wensleydale, as this book will show you.

Secondly, the cheesemaking practices referred to in this section typically refer to those employed by people making cheese for smaller markets – that is, for people who share their level of adoration for the product. Having read this section, we hope you discover what the art of making cheese is all about, and even, perhaps, to try making it yourself.

The basic cheesemaking process can be summed up by the diagram below:

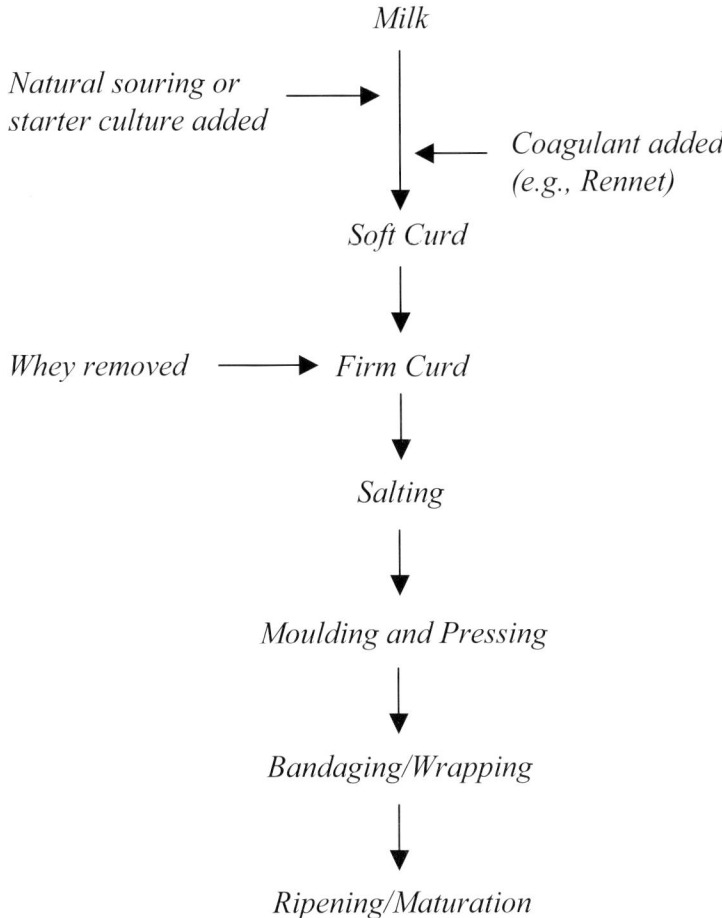

Let's take a closer look at each of the stages involved, beginning with milk.

Milk

This is of course the fundamental ingredient of any cheese. Later in this chapter we'll talk about the different types of milk that can be used and the characteristics of each one. For now, let's look at its unique properties that make cheesemaking possible. These are:

1. Its ability to clot or *coagulate* to form a solid curd. This is because it contains a protein called casein, which separates into a solid when rennet is added or the milk turns acidic.

2. Its ability to sour and become more acidic. This is due to lactose, or *milk-sugar* as it is also known. Bacteria within the milk feed on lactose and in doing so produce lactic acid, thus increasing the acidity of the milk.

3. Its fat content. This varies in quantity according to the milk type, but in all cases contributes greatly to the flavour, aroma and body in mature cheeses. Higher fat content usually means a softer cheese; conversely, milk with a low percentage of fat will result in a harder type.

4. Protein. Remember Little Miss Muffet? Well in scientific terms, whilst sitting on her tuffet, she ate casein and whey proteins. If you've ever made yourself a mug of hot milk and left it standing for a little while, that awful skin that forms at the surface is composed of whey proteins. The curd (or casein) is what forms the bulk of cheese, whereas the whey is generally discarded as a waste product. Without the protein content in milk, the separation of (and indeed, presence of) curds and whey couldn't happen.

Souring

Traditionally this was left to happen naturally, however it was unreliable in regard to consistency and posed a health risk if not monitored carefully. Nowadays a starter culture is usually added to accelerate the rate of souring and produce a much higher yield through less wastage.

Also at this stage bacteria can be added to later break down the curd from the inside outwards. It is these bacteria that are responsible for the bloomy white rinds you'll see on a Brie, for example, or the characteristic blue veining in Stilton. These blue streaks have often been enhanced by extra exposure to air, when the cheese is pierced with skewers to allow it penetrate deep inside.

Rennet

This is the ingredient responsible for turning the milk into a solid. Rennet is an enzyme found in the stomach lining of cows, or is sometimes extracted from plants. This latter form is used in the production of vegetarian cheese.

Soft and Firm Curd

Having added rennet, the milk begins to solidify within a relatively short period of time. Once this has occurred, it is cut (usually into small cubes) and the leftover liquid (whey) is drained. How much of this is drained depends on how hard the cheese is likely to be; leaving a higher amount of whey will result in a softer cheese whereas thorough draining causes a harder end product.

Salting

Four methods exist according to what type of cheese is being made:

- Hard Cheese – salt is added during milling for three reasons: to stop acid developing further, to aid in flavour, and to act as a preserving agent in the finished cheese.

- Soft Cheese – rubbing salt onto the outside of these smaller cheeses a couple of times assists in the formation of its rind. The salt is absorbed through the cheese during a short time.

- Blue Veined Cheese – with these varieties the salt is usually added to the curd before moulding (see next stage), though in some cases it is added during or after the process.

- Brine Salted Cheese – following moulding, these cheeses are placed in a saltwater solution strong enough to float it, during which they absorb the salt throughout before being allowed to dry.

Moulding and Pressing

This involves consolidating the curds into the shape in which the cheese will be matured, and ultimately sold. The moulds are initially lined with cheesecloth before the curds are added to help additional whey drainage. *Progressive* pressure is then applied over time to force out the whey and ensure it does not become trapped inside the cheese. How long the cheese is pressed for again has much bearing on how hard the final product will be. With harder varieties such as Cheddar, scalding hot water is poured over the cheese following moulding and pressing to harden the protein and effectively begin the rind-forming process.

Bandaging

Traditionally the bandaging (using cheesecloth) is wrapped tightly around the cheese from top to bottom, and then stitched into place. When buying certain varieties such as Cheddar or Red Leicester, look for the faint criss-cross indentations on the rind that signify it has been wrapped in cheesecloth.

Ripening and Maturation

Having passed through all of the above phases, the new cheese is taken to the storage area where it will begin to acquire its true characteristics. Bacteria – either added to the curd or naturally present – will ripen the cheese through the action of enzymes. Maturation and ripening times vary according to type of cheese and can be anything from a couple of weeks to three years!

And that's about it, in a simplified form, of course. Bear in mind that whole books have been written on the scientific processes behind cheesemaking, and this is *not* one of them. Our aim in detailing this is to help you understand the steps in between having a bottle of milk and piece of cheese.

So Many Cheeses ...

There are several different ways of classifying types of cheese. You could separate them by the type of milk they were made with, by their flavour, fat content, or most commonly by their texture. This book will classify them using both their milk type and their texture. You may find that many of the cheeses overlap classifications as they sometimes change their characteristics throughout its life.

Unlike wines, there are no concrete classifications for cheeses in regard to their composition. Although in some cases it is obvious to which category a cheese belongs, sometimes it can be a lot trickier to determine, as there are so many variables. For example, what some people may class as a 'hard' cheese may be classed by others as 'semi-hard' or 'semi-soft'. So ultimately, remember that the categorising process is a personal issue and that you are free to assume your own views as and when you like.

For the purpose of this book (and after much debate!), we have settled upon four categories, detailed below. You may find that other experts have created many more – sometimes as many as eight – but for simplicity's sake, four will suffice.

Soft

Examples of soft cheeses include Somerset Brie, Tymsboro, and types such as Cottage Cheese and Cream Cheese. These types are squidgy (and runny at room temperature) in texture and spread easily on your favourite accompaniment. These types of cheeses have a high water content as they retain up to 85% of their moisture during maturation. Due to this they are more attractive to microbes, which cause them to ripen faster, compared to the hard cheeses that can take months. Of course, it also means that they perish sooner!

Semi-Soft

A slightly lower moisture content is the reason behind these cheeses' firmer texture. Gubbeen and Milleens, both from Ireland, fit into this category, which is closely related to that above. Cheeses within this classification undergo a washing process which aids in keeping the rind moist and also encourages the fermentation process.

Semi-Hard

These cheeses retain around 45% of their moisture during maturation; therefore they are not as firm as the harder varieties. However they do have a stable composition – you can't spread these on your water biscuits! If you do, have the vacuum handy. These cheeses differ from soft cheeses as they can either be eaten young or several months old depending on the type of cheese produced. The semi-hard cheese category contains some of the widely used varieties of cheese. A few popular examples include Sage Derby, the infamous Cheddar and Shropshire Blue; you can find out a little more about them later in the book!

Semi-hard (and hard too) cheeses are pressed during the production stage and the more whey extracted during this process means the moisture content falls too.

Hard

These cheeses can be either cooked and unpressed, or uncooked and pressed. They are usually aged for up to a year in a humid environment, though some types such as the world renowned Parmiganio Regiano is matured for a whopping 24 months.

The UK is not really a producer of this type of cheese, and in fact you will be hard pressed (excuse the pun) to find any varieties within our shores. Italy is renowned for its selection, with choices including Parmesan (mentioned above), Romano and Pecorino.

A low water content of up to 30% means that cheese falling into this category keeps well and is ideal for grating or other cooking purposes.

What to Look For: Determining a Good Cheese

So, you've planned that dinner party and are in the midst of buying all the necessities. One of your stopping points for your pièce de resistance (or your cheese board) is the counter at the supermarket, or if you find yourself with sufficient time, the local dairy and retail outlet. Let's assume we're visiting the latter, though the following hints will serve you perfectly well in any situation.

Upon entering the shop you find yourself swamped with cheeses of every shape, colour and size. And the smell! Believe it or not, it can actually become rather appealing, as we found out through repeated visits to such places. Covering every useable space is either a cheese of some variety or something closely related. Shops such as these can be real treasure troves. In fact we came across a delightful home-made hot pepper and onion chutney just the other day when visiting our local dairy. Anyway, we digress …

But where to start? All those illusions of just popping in to pick up any old piece that looks reasonable have just gone out of the window. Well, don't despair. The following guidelines will provide you with some useful information to help prevent what should be an enjoyable experience turning into a nightmare.

Firstly, don't be put off by the person behind the counter. Whilst it is of course true that they are there to make profit, and therefore they won't want to scare you away, look a bit further beyond this. All the people we have spoken to running such shops have been enthusiastic, passionate and genuinely helpful about their subject and only too willing to help you out. Don't be afraid to ask them questions – after all, that's what they're there for! And you'll find that you will be able to sample their wares before you purchase them, just in case you're dubious about buying a whole piece of something that you've never tried before. Now you have no excuse not to try them all out!

And so to the cheese. Firstly, bear in mind that the owner will usually have selected their specific products themselves, and in doing so will have endeavoured to buy only what they consider to be the best from each batch. This already has its advantages for you in that no cheese in the shop should taste unlike it is supposed to, or even (dare we say it), bad. It has already been graded and accepted by a professional.

You'll be able to gather a vast amount of knowledge about the cheese simply by looking at the rind. Softer varieties should have a smooth, untarnished 'bloom', free of blemishes or other mould growth. Harder ones will have a tough, darker rind with no cracks. Should this not be the case with either type, there is a good chance the cheese is not suitable for consumption.

Where the interior of the cheese is visible, look for any more signs of cracking on harder types; this will signify that the cheese has dried out and subsequently deteriorated in quality. Types such as Cheddar that are darker near the rind or cut edges should be avoided as it means they have nearly dried out. A very shiny or oily appearance could mean the opposite – that is, it has not been kept in cool enough conditions and has 'sweated'. Again, this will affect the overall flavour and quality of the product, so stay away. Remember, however, that even the hardest of cheeses should be moist. If the interior of a softer cheese such as Brie seems chalky and pale instead of golden and smooth, it will probably mean it is not yet fully ripened. Whilst this in itself does not make it inedible, unless you are happy to wait for it to become mature, it is better to find one that has already done so.

Of course, the shop owner will assist you in making your decisions, and, decidedly content with your purchases, you head home …

Later that evening, having suitably impressed your guests with the meal so far, out comes the cheese board. Here's a few tips to help you and your guests get the most from it and truly make the meal a memorable experience:

- Serve the milder cheeses first as the stronger ones will overwhelm them if eaten the other way round.
- Eat slowly and allow the full flavours to develop. The point of eating this course is not to make sure you're full, but to savour and enjoy the product. Letting each one linger on the palate helps to do this immensely.
- Think carefully about what you are experiencing at each stage of eating; what it tastes like initially, what flavours start to develop, how strong it tastes, and depth of finish – does it linger or disappear dramatically?
- Assess the different textures too: feel how smooth some are compared to those with a grainy or chalky feel in the mouth. Note how some will literally melt on your tongue whereas others will take some time to break down. This is all part of forming your personal favourites (and those that you don't like so much).
- For those guests who are not exactly clued up on the subject, assure them that the aroma they will no doubt be turning their noses up at is quite deliberate and does *not* signify it has perished!

Once you start to feel a little more confident in tasting cheese, it's inevitable that you'll decide upon certain types as your personal favourites. Don't worry, however, if you find that these vary in flavour from week to week – you're not going mad! It's actually because the taste can vary within the same type according to which batch it has come from. Now, whilst these differences are not dramatic, it is a common occurrence. Besides, if you can distinguish them, you're well on the way to increasing your cheese know-how. Well done!

Storing the Cheese

It goes without saying that cheese is a perishable product and therefore, to maintain its quality, it must be looked after properly. If you are unsure as to how long you can keep your chosen variety for, remember this general rule of thumb: the harder the cheese is, the longer it will retain its freshness.

Temperature

Cheese should ideally be stored between 5°C and 10°C, that is, in a cool environment. Those with a cellar should consider themselves lucky – they are perfect for keeping cheeses, as the temperature maintained by a refrigerator tends to be too cool. For those of you still living in the Stone Age (you know who you are!), your cave should work just fine. However, the majority of us will no doubt find ourselves having to make do with a fridge, so we will concentrate a little more on that instead.

Because the fridge can often be a bit too chilly for cheese (usually between 2°C and 6°C), try to find room at the bottom, which is the warmest area. Try at all costs to keep it away from strong foods whilst it is in there, as cheese has an amazing ability to absorb flavours from its surroundings, and change its taste altogether. This is obviously of greater significance when storing milder cheeses with a more subtle taste, as they are more susceptible to acquiring a new flavour. And we're not sure about you, but we'd prefer our Brie without that hint of tuna …

Packaging/Wrapping

A constant debate rages as to how cheese should be wrapped whilst in storage. Some argue that it should be tightly wrapped in cling film or foil, perhaps even placed in an airtight container, to help retain its moisture. Others claim cheese must be allowed to 'breathe' and should therefore be kept loosely in waxed cheese paper or foil. The use of cling film can cause the cheese to sweat due to excessive moisture and this in turn accelerates mould growth; leaving it with insufficient wrapping will cause it to dry out and crack. Our friends across the Channel have been known to wrap their cheese in vine leaves, which strikes a happy medium for both parties. If you don't have a vineyard for a back garden though (and we don't), try adding green vegetable leaves or stalks such as celery within a loose wrapping to help retain moisture and still allow breathing. It's all about keeping a balance!

Another hint: when re-wrapping cheese, use fresh packaging each time to inhibit the spread of bacteria, especially onto the newly cut surface.

Picture this: you've just arrived home after another long day at work and rather than spend the remainder of the day cooking, you decide on a simple cheese dish – say, Welsh rarebit. Upon opening your fridge you find that a piece of Cheddar that's been lurking in there for far longer than you'd care to remember has, ahem, evolved. Put simply, it's covered in mould. So what do you do? Most people wouldn't hesitate to throw it in the bin. However, try cutting half an inch off each side where the growth has occurred and your cheese should be fine.

NOTE: we do advise that you use common sense in doing this – a piece that is completely beleaguered with mould belongs in the bin. It's as simple as that! Further to this, you can slow the process of bacterial growth by handling the cheese as little as possible and using clean utensils to cut it with.

To Freeze or not to Freeze ...

Whilst this is possible, we don't recommend it, as the main drawback is it will cause a deterioration in texture and cause it to crumble. This of course is no problem if you intend to cook with it, as it does however retain its flavour. Bear in mind that harder, stronger cheeses are better to freeze than softer varieties due to their composition and robust flavour. You should also consider the following points when freezing cheese:

- Freeze in blocks no greater than 250g (about half a pound if you refuse to go metric!). This ensures the cheese freezes evenly and faster, as slow freezing will cause it to become even more crumbly upon thawing.

- Unlike storing cheese in a cellar or fridge, make sure it is tightly wrapped using foil or film to help retain moisture. This will again help to prevent it becoming too crumbly when it is defrosted.

- When you are ready to defrost, do so in the fridge and eat as soon as possible – don't forget to make sure it still comes up to room temperature though.

- Don't despair if your cheese appears mottled or discoloured at first when you remove it from the freezer. Once defrosted, it should return to its original colour.

- Cheese from the freezer is best suited to cooking rather than appearing on a cheese board. This is because its appearance and texture will have suffered the most from the freezing process; it's crumbly and not really presentable enough. So get out those fondue sets that you thought you'd never use again, they're coming back in fashion you know (you heard it here first!).

- Never refreeze cheese. As with any food, it isn't safe and will affect its quality over time.

Did you know? It is possible to store cheese by coating it in paraffin. Dipping it or painting about four layers onto the surface will help to preserve your cheese almost indefinitely.

Making a Great Cheeseboard

Choosing your cheese varieties ...

Cheese is a living product which changes daily. When buying cheese for your dinner party you need to make sure that the cheese is going to be ripe when you serve it. So when buying Brie on a Wednesday for a dinner party on Saturday make sure that it is a little under ripened (slightly chalky in the middle) so that by the time it comes to your dinner party it will be at its best. Obviously don't buy cheese that is perfect for eating now if you are going to be storing it for a long time. If you have any problems telling at what stage of ripening a cheese is, then just ask the assistant behind the counter. If they can't tell you, then we would probably suggest looking for your cheese elsewhere.

You need to follow a few simple steps when choosing the right cheeses to serve on your cheeseboard. It's essential to offer a good variety of cheeses – those of different textures such as soft and semi-soft, and also the different milk types such as cow and sheep. To make it more interesting try and buy some cheeses with different shapes and colours. With that as a starting point the rest should be relatively easy. The aim is to impress your guests with your chosen variety of cheeses and their different textures and intensities of flavours, not to confuse them by having too many.

Depending on the size of the cheese board and the number of guests, only present 4 to 6 cheeses, otherwise the board may appear cluttered. You also need to consider how much cheese to buy; we would suggest allocating around 45 to 60 grams of cheese per person depending how large the main meal was, and if you are going to have a dessert.

If you do not live near a specialist food shop, good cheese can be hard to come by, so don't fret if you can't get a good selection. Just try and find two or three really good cheeses and use them. Some of the trendy restaurants in London are only serving one cheese to their customers and changing it daily, so don't worry!

Boards ...

Usually cheeses are presented on a cheeseboard, however there are several options open to you if you feel a little adventurous. There are no rules as to what makes a good board: some like to use a normal wooden model, others like to use slate, marble, baskets, or even a piece of drift wood can work! As long as it is flat so that it is easy to cut and it's hygienic, then give it a try.

Presenting the cheese ...

This is where you can become creative or as simplistic as you like. As a practical approach some people like to serve cheese on several small boards as this will prevent the smells and flavours from one cheese combining with others. Other people simply use one large board and consciously try to keep the cheeses away from each other. If you use the *clock* method of presenting, where cheeses are arranged from lightest and mildest to the richer and stronger in flavour in a clockwise fashion, then the mixing of flavours will be less of an issue.

The cheese should be cut in either blocks or wedges depending on the type of cheese (see our section on cutting and slicing). If they are small enough, you can also present whole cheeses on a board which look very impressive, such as a Pentland or a mini Stilton. Beware though – some people consider these to be inferior in flavour and quality to the standard-sized ones, despite there being no proof of this! Although you may not want to eat the rind on some of the cheeses you should leave it on when presenting. You can tell a lot about a cheese from its rind: it has its own persona and adds a touch of character to the display.

Once you have arranged your cheeses on the board then you can begin to add a little decoration. Remember not to dress it up too much, as you are meant to be presenting the cheese. Virtually anything can be used to decorate the cheese board and here are a few ideas:

- Fruit can be added, as long as you make sure that it is fresh, juicy and full of flavour. It also looks great if you can obtain them with their leaves and stalks still attached. Pears, figs and grapes (especially the small dried ones still in bunches) are ideal.
- If you can't find any fresh seasonal fruit then use dried varieties.
- Some like to use rustic decorations such as oak leaves, chestnuts and pinecones.
- Flowers are a fantastic way of brightening up a cheese board, but be careful that pollen does not contaminate the cheese.
- You could also use a stick or two of celery and a carrot, or a bunch of herbs fresh from the garden.

After you have finished your beautiful presentation don't put it in the fridge – just cover it with a damp clean tea-towel and leave it on the side so that it will stay at room temperature (but not for too long).

When to bring it out ...

There is much debate as to when you should present your cheese board at a dinner party. Usually here in Britain we would present it at the end of the meal, perhaps with an after-dinner drink such as port. Some like to serve cheese prior to the dessert as this helps in the transition from savoury to sweeter flavours (usually restaurant owners and the French). Others like to serve it before the main meal as a starter. Some fanatical cheese lovers merely do away with the dessert and replace it with a good cheese board as it acts as a palate cleanser, very much like a sorbet would.

Accompaniments …

Although cheese is great on its own it is also nice to serve a few accompaniments. There are literally hundreds of them to choose from and we have selected a few of our favourites:

Crackers – These little beauties come in many different shapes and sizes and they are ideal for eating with cheese, acting as a perfect base for virtually any variety.

Bread – There is nothing better than going to the bakery early in the morning and picking up a fresh loaf of crusty farmhouse bread; it makes the perfect companion for cheese as it is simple, easy and tastes divine. Breads with wholegrain, multigrain or poppy seeds have a rustic and earthy taste, ideal for Cheddar, Double Gloucester and Leicester, those classic farmhouse cheeses. If you are feeling a little more adventurous you may like to purchase some flavoured speciality bread. One little gem that we have found is Elizabeth Botham's Plum Bread, which can be found at the Chatsworth Farm shop in the Peak District. This bread is ideal with most cheeses – try in particular with Cashel Blue or Sharpham's, or something which is flavoursome and packs a punch (information about these cheeses can be found in later sections of the book). A crusty French loaf is perfect for the softer cheeses – try it with Brie and you'll find a wonderful contrast in textures. Also, if you can find it, try eating olive bread with any cheese made from ewe's milk, such as Berkswell.

Meats – These also go well as an accompaniment with cheese, such as Italian Parma ham, proscuittio or other cured meats. They are ideal as they are soft in texture, and have a distinctive flavour that is often slightly salty in contrast to the cheese. Other cured meats that are popular to eat with cheese include the air-dried beef from Switzerland, Bundnerfleisch; Serrano, a dry-cured Spanish ham is another fine choice with its sweet, delicate flavour. Try experimenting with smoked cured hams or pastrami and the stronger flavoured cheeses such Quickes Extra Mature Cheddar. Another good point to remember is that, like cheese, all meats should be served at room temperature in order to extract the most flavour.

Olives – Some people love them whereas others hate them, yet they go great with cheese. The nice thing about olives is that that there are many different types which can be bought pre-dressed with an array of flavours, or you may even like to dress your own. Our favourites include:

- Almond stuffed olives with extra virgin walnut oil dressed with coriander and garlic, which go particularly well with any goat's cheese.
- Moroccan black olives in balsamic vinegar with a rosemary and honey dressing, which are sweeter and ideal with rich cheeses such as Wexford Stilton, or Cashel Blue.

Nuts – These are ideal with any cheese; we particularly like toasting almonds and eating them with cheeses made from goat's or ewe's milk. Other nuts you may like to consider include walnuts, toasted hazelnuts and unflavoured peanuts.

Membrillo (Quince Paste) – Membrillo is a jelly or paste made from quince, a medieval shrub which produces fruit of the same name resembling a large yellow pear. The word *Membrillo* comes from the Latin word *Melimelum*, which translates into *honey apple*. This jelly is very sweet, soft and fragrant and can be likened to cranberry sauce. Although it is traditionally eaten with the hard Spanish cheese Manchego, it is ideal with most of the stronger hard cheeses produced here in England such as Cheddar, as the sweetness contrasts with the salty sharpness of the cheese. To serve, you should slice the cheese thinly and place an even thinner slice of Membrillo on the top; simply eat it like that or put it on a plain cracker, perfect!

Cutting and Slicing Cheese

Firstly, we want to acknowledge that this is not something you may want to pay particular attention to every time you cut cheese. However, on occasions where you deem it necessary to present it properly and make it look attractive, slicing cheese is a fundamental issue. There are various methods attributed to different types and shapes of cheese that have been used for quite some time now, all of which not only aid the presentation, but will prevent you from ruining the quality of the original piece if you are not using it all at once.

Try to cut your cheese whilst it is still cold (leave Brie to reach room temperature before cutting it and you'll see why!), and use a sharp, heavy knife – the extra weight will help you slice through the harder types. You may also wish to use a cheese wire for the really hard varieties and this not only prevents you from ruining a knife blade but is undoubtedly safer too.

The aim in cutting cheese is to ensure an even balance between the inside and the rind. It's also about making sure everybody has an equal share of the three components; rind, body and heart. This lets people appreciate the full appeal of the cheese they are about to eat, and gain a true insight into its flavour as these three parts more often than not taste different – especially the rind, which tends to have the strongest flavour.

Wheels and Truckles

Cut these into wedges. A straightforward method of doing this is to imagine that the whole piece is made up of layers, about one inch thick. Slice a wedge one at a time from a layer and only begin a new one when you have cut all the wedges from the previous layer. Try to keep the cut as smooth and flat as you can.

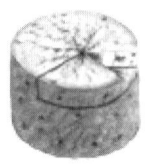

These large wedges can be cut into smaller ones if you prefer, and the same also applies to any cheese that is triangular in shape, though this is not something you will come across often.

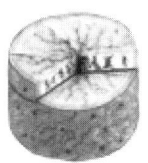

Rectangular and Square Pieces

First make a diagonal incision from one corner to the other, on any side if it is square, on one of the ends if it is rectangular. Then slice down as if you were cutting a full size piece; the incision made previously will mean you actually end up with two triangles of cheese. This is handy if you are only using one piece at a time as you can wrap the other back up with the original piece exactly as it was before it was cut.

Pyramidal Pieces

Probably the most awkward to slice but fortunately quite rare, there is no one method for slicing. The general rule of thumb is to always slice in the same direction from the centre, whatever method you choose.

At the Table

Once at the table, dispose of the heavy chef's knives; they belong in the kitchen and will appear somewhat daunting to someone wanting to cut a small portion for themselves. Smaller, more attractive cheese knives are far more suited to this task, and if you really want to create an impression there are several models available according to the type of cheese you want to cut. Consider these points before you decide which knife/knives to buy:

- It is not compulsory to buy several different knives for each cheese you're sampling. Types of knife do exist that will take care of cheeses ranging from soft to hard. The *Classic Black* model by Wüsthof Trident is an excellent example of this.

- For cutting softer cheese, invest in a knife that has etching or cut-outs in the blade (such as the *5.5in. Cheese Knife* by Global). This will help prevent the cheese from sticking to the blade and creating a mess.

- Harder cheeses can be dealt with effortlessly by using a knife such as the *5.5in Cheese Knife* by Henckels which is specially made to cope with firmer textures. The *Fork-Tip Cheese Knife*, also by Henckels, is also useful for sliding pieces onto your plate or cracker as well as cutting.

- For harder varieties it is also useful to have a 'stepped' blade that is lower than the handle. This will reduce the chances of you or your guests rapping their knuckles on the platter if the blade moves downwards quicker than anticipated. We learnt that the hard way!

- Want something a bit more novel or just trying to cut costs? Try dental floss for cutting softer cheeses (though flavoured varieties may not be quite so appropriate!).

Once the cheese is on your plate, or if you are all helping yourselves from one larger platter, it is more or less up to you how you choose to cut it. Obviously some will be more straightforward than others, so don't worry if you find the Brie is a little tricky to manoeuvre between dish and mouth/bread. Do try and keep it looking presentable however – even if this takes a little practice!

Cheese and ... Drinks

Pairing any cheese with a drink can be very exciting especially as there are so many combinations and so many different types of flavours which can be induced. The pairing of cheese and a drink is very much about personal taste and preference. There are a few ways in which you can go about it: firstly, you may decide to just give it a go and pair combinations which you feel may work well together; secondly, you can do a little background reading on the characteristics of the cheese and drink, and then pair them yourself; lastly, you may decide that it's all too complicated and the easiest option would be to find out what the experts say and then copy them – you never know, it may spur you on to become a little more adventurous!

Most people think only of cheese pairing with wine and port, though as a dedicated cheese lover you will also want to try accompanying it with other fortified varieties such as vermouth and sherry, whilst also not forgetting beer, ale, stout, juices, and scrumpy. The choice is yours.

Let's start with the basics, cheese and wine pairing. An old myth that seems to be floating around is that all red wines go well with any cheese – this is not the case. Pairing any cheese with a wine takes a little bit of planning, as both flavours can be complex and delicate, however the basics are straightforward enough. Knowing if you have got it right is in the testing. When pairing the two you first have to decide whether you are looking for contrasting or complementing flavours. Here are a few pointers to help you along the way:

- Have a go at pairing cheese with a drink which will complement it, and then try and find one which contrasts it.

- When tasting cheese with wine try a little of the wine first to identify its strong characteristics, as the flavour of the cheese will be stronger and will cause the wine's taste to change. When tasting wine look for and note its acidity, flavours, evaluate how it feels, what it reminds you of and its finish. By tasting it first you will appreciate how the cheese affects the change on the palate.
- Do not go over the top and try matching too many drinks with several different varieties of cheese as it will be difficult to distinguish between different flavours.
- Try to stick to two or three different beverages and cheeses to taste.
- Note that using up a half empty bottle of wine from the night before with your cheese board will usually result in failure.
- Opposites often do attract – combinations such as port and Stilton or even a little apricot dessert wine and Stilton, for example. If you are really adventurous you could try Somerset Brie and Brandy or the 12 month old mature Kerrygold Cheddar and Guinness (we have chosen an Irish cheese to keep with the theme).
- As a very rough guide we would recommend fruity reds and light white wines with mild cheeses; we would suggest you go for a Riesling, Zinfandel or a young Chardonnay. Mature cheeses go well with full-bodied reds such as a Cabernet Sauvignon or Syrah. The blue cheeses are ideal with sweet and fortified wines such as port or sherry, and also a white desert wine.
- Try to eat locally produced cheeses and wines together; not only will it help out the local economy, but it will act as an interesting talking point. However, do not assume that just because cheeses and your selected beverage are produced within the same region they will automatically go together!

Hang on a minute ...

There is of course one situation you may find yourself in when you should never taste cheese. It may seem strange, but you should never taste cheese when you are tasting wine. We are sure that all you wine connoisseurs are aware that cheese has the tendency to enhance the flavour and iron out the roughness of some of the younger, shall we say, less refined, wines. This is good news if you are enjoying the two together, but it will not give a true impression of the wine if you want to appreciate the flavour. A top tip is never purchase wine from a merchant who gives you cheese to taste with it as they are probably trying to hide something.

32 Things You Never Knew You Wanted To Know About Cheese

1. Charles de Gaulle once remarked about France, "How can you govern a nation that has 246 varieties of cheese?"

2. The average American will eat half a ton of cheese in a lifetime.

3. Rennin, the enzyme obtained from the fourth stomach of a cow and used chiefly in the manufacture of cheese, is capable of coagulating more than 25,000 times its weight of fresh milk.

4. As of 1988, the U.S. census bureau determined that a stunning 13% of the population believe that some portion of the earth's moon is actually comprised of cheese.

5. To make 1 pound of cheese, a dairy cow must first eat 3 pounds of food.

6. The world's largest cheese was manufactured by the farmers in and around the Ottawa Valley in an effort to promote Canadian Cheese. It was transported to the Chicago World's fair, where after display it was cut up and sold in small pieces to patrons of the fair. Anyone could come to Andrew Jackson's public parties at the White House, and just about everyone did! At his last one, a wheel of cheese weighing 1,400 lbs. was eaten in two hours. The White House smelled of cheese for weeks.

7. The ancient French cheese, Mariolles, was so pungent that heat waves emanated from it.

8. France eats the most cheese, per capita, than any other country in the world. It has 216 different varieties of cheese.

9. The U.S. produces more cheese than any other country – 6,717,000,000 pounds a year.

10. Wisconsin produces more cheese than any other US state – 1,913,681,000 pounds a year.

11. Skunks absolutely love cheese. Cheddar is their favourite. They will follow cheddar anywhere.

12. In 1987, a 1400 year old piece of cheese was dug up in Ireland and is still edible!

13. Cheese was once used as money!

14. "Big cheese" and "big wheel" are medieval terms of envious respect for those who could afford to buy whole wheels of cheese at a time, an expense few could enjoy. Both these terms are often used sarcastically today.

15. When England was a province of Rome, the city of Cheshire was noted for its fine cheese. The Romans built a wall around the town to protect it. Cheshire cheese was made in a mould shaped like a cat, later made famous as the smiling feline in Lewis Carroll's Alice in Wonderland.

16. The Food and Drug Administration advises pregnant women to avoid soft cheeses, including queso blanco, feta, Brie, Camembert, and blue-veined cheeses, such as Roquefort. Certain soft cheeses can carry the bacterium Listeria, which poses a risk to an unborn child.

17. Bel paese, caciocavallo, gjetost, herkimer, liederkranz, liptaur, mysost, sapsago, and trappist are all varieties of cheese.

18. Gjetost is the national cheese of Norway, and its name means "goat" and "cheese," though it is now commonly made of cow's milk.

19. Of all cheese customs, one of the more unusual was that of the "groaning cheese." Years ago in Europe, a prospective father would nibble on a huge chunk of cheese while awaiting the home birth of his child. Instead of pacing outside the bedroom door, the father would eat from the centre of the cheese until a large hole had been gnawed out. Later, his newborn infant was ceremoniously passed through the hole.

20. In Britain, the first instance of a demand for film censorship came from an outraged cheese industry in 1898. Charles Urban had released one of his scientific films taken through a microscope which revealed the unappealing bacterial activity in a piece of Stilton.

21. French law stipulates that to be called "Roquefort," a cheese must come only from that village in France, but the name is used, imitated, and abused widely.

22. The first law to protect the cheese industry was enacted in 1411, when Charles VI gave the people of Roquefort "the monopoly of curing cheese as has been done in the caves of Roquefort village since time immemorial."

23. Victorian England foods hid many poisons. Sulfate of copper was put in pickles. Red lead gave Gloucester cheese its red hue. Lead was added to wine and cider, and was extensively used and accumulative in effect, often resulting in chronic gastritis and

fatal food poisoning.

24. British households spend about 1.5 billion pounds a year on cheese for family consumption.

25. Highly prized, Saanenkaese is a cheese made in Switzerland in small quantities. This Swiss grating cheese is matured for up to seven years.

26. Cheddar varieties account for 57% of volume of cheese sold in England

27. According to the British Cheese Board, cheese appears in 32% of British lunchboxes and sandwiches. Cheese on toast and other bread uses account for more than 60% of all meal occasions featuring cheese.

28. In the cheesemaking industry, the interior of a cheese is called the paste.

29. Real Roquefort cheese is made from ewe's milk under strict regulations. It must be aged for at least two months in the limestone caves of Cambalou in the South of France.

30. It requires about ten pounds of milk to make one pound of natural cheese.

31. The higher the fat content in a cheese, the faster it will melt.

32. "Ol' cheese" is an Aussie slang expression for "Mother."

The Cheeses

Having given some background knowledge of cheese, and guided you through the process of choosing, storing, cutting and eating, we are now proud to present 43 carefully selected varieties.

We have chosen the 43 because we feel they represent the best of what British cheese has to offer. The first 30 are fully described; due to limitations of time and space, the remainder, while equally worthy of a mention, are covered in somewhat less detail.

One thing is for sure – they are all unique and very tasty!

Appleby's Cheshire

Cheshire is thought to be the oldest British cheese. It is mentioned in the Domesday book (1086) and probably dates back to Roman times. Genuine Cheshire is said to be made with the milk from cattle grazed on the salty pastures of the Cheshire plain in Cheshire, Shropshire and Clywd. This is a semi-hard cheese and is made from cow's milk.

Appearance:
This cheese has a moist and crumbly texture. The rind has a grey tint to it.

Nose:
This cheese has a beautiful aroma. It is fresh on the nose and the rind has a barnyard aroma.

Taste:
This cheese, when matured for four to six months, gives a pleasant light, salty flavour. This flavour becomes more pronounced with age. A lively, lightly acidic flavour with a flaky texture. The white Cheshire is sharp and it has a somewhat salty tang.

Overall Opinion of the Cheese:
It is a fabulous cheese with distinct flavours that is a true testament to the long process involved in making it. An old cheese but still one of the best.

Production: Appleby's is made with raw milk, cloth wrapping and a vegetarian rennet. They make it using what is known as a 'slower recipe'. This means less starter is used as a catalyst. Obviously the difficulty with this is that the slower the recipe, the more chance of things going wrong. But this also means that there is more chance of a higher quality cheese in the end. The levels of wastage are also higher. This Cheshire cheese takes only two to three hours to make. The morning milk is added to the previous evening's milk, and after coagulation the curds are scalded in the whey for about 40 minutes. The whey is drained off very quickly while the cheese-maker cuts the curds and then tears it into small pieces. It is then salted, milled and put into moulds to be pressed for 24 to 48 hours. Appleby's still use unpasteurised milk and bandage their cheese in the traditional way using cloths dipped in lard. Ripening takes from 4 to 8 weeks but cheeses can be kept for well over a year.

Eating and drink: This cheese makes an excellent eating experience as well as first-class rarebits and soufflés. It has the reputation of being one of the very best cooking cheeses in Europe and was renowned during King Charles I's day. Previously this Cheshire cheese has been enjoyed with raspberry jam, and a really mature cheese with gooseberry jam. Wines, which this particular cheese complements, include: Fleurie - Chapelle des Bois (Beaujolais) and Pinot Noir - Cougars Moon (California).

Storage: To enjoy this cheese at its best you should keep it in a cardboard box in an unheated room and wrapped in waxed paper with a piece of cling film over the cut surface of the cheese only. If an unheated room is not available then the salad drawer at the bottom of your fridge will do, but the cheese won't keep as well.

Produced: Appleby Family, Appleby Farm, Hawkestone, Shropshire.

Recommended:
Appleby's Smoked Cheshire – Before smoking a cheese, it is cut into four wheels. This enables the smoky flavour to fully penetrate. The Appleby's smoke their Cheshire cheeses over oak bark, to give the rich distinctive flavour. The rind becomes darker brown and has a fabulous smoky aroma. Interestingly, the paste becomes a little paler.

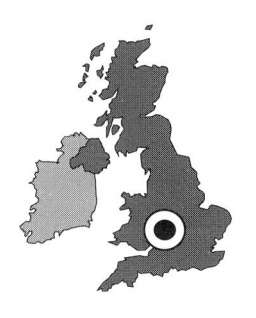

Red Cheshire was made by accident – it was used to show the difference between Cheshire from Wales and London and it is now more popular!

Beenleigh Blue

Beenleigh Blue has been around since 1970. The cheese was developed as the producers were looking for new markets for their ewe's milk. It is a semi-soft farmhouse cheese produced using unpasteurised ewe's milk. It has a rough, sticky, natural rind that has grey and white patches. Beenleigh is produced on the Sharpham estate in Devon by Robin Congdon, who, whilst working on the farm, got a chance to milk the ewes which inspired him to make yoghurt – it wasn't long until he was making cheese. The cheese is organic and the milk is provided by two flocks that graze on the doorstep of the dairy.

Appearance:
The paste is very creamy, pale yellow in colour with bluey green veining.

Nose:
It has the typical nose of a blue cheese, with a musty, fungi smelling crust.

Taste:
The texture of the cheese is velvety and rich; the cheese has an underlying sweetness with ewe's milk undertones and the

saltiness that is typical of blue cheeses.

Overall opinion of cheese:
This is an outstanding ewe's milk cheese, which has a close firm texture and tangy long lasting flavours.

Production: The milk is heat treated for thirty minutes before the cheesemaking process begins. The Penicillium Roquefortii culture is added and it is left for around forty five minutes – the time here depends on the season as this greatly affects the quality of the milk. The curds are broken by hand and packed into moulds, and stay in these moulds for two days. The surfaces of the cheese are then coated in salt and the holes that allow the cheese to blue are spiked. Once bluing has taken place the cheeses are wrapped in foil to prevent the rind from forming. Affinage for this cheese takes around six months. The cheeses are made from January to July and are therefore available to buy from September to February.

Eating and drink: Beenleigh is excellent enjoyed by itself, or great for cooking sauces, and is a great addition to any salad. It does, of course, deserve a place on your cheese board and is best enjoyed with a glass of mead or sweet cider. For those that prefer wine, a Merlot Cabernet is a perfect accompaniment to this cheese.

Storage: The cheese remains in its cylindrical shape and needs to be stored in the fridge until required. When needed, it should be removed from the fridge and allowed to come to room temperature for at least an hour. Eating straight from the fridge will mean that the flavours are not developed and the texture not ripened to its best. It should be stored in foil or more appropriately in cheese paper.

Produced: This cheese is produced in Devon by Robin Congdon on the Sharpham Estate in Totnes.

Stockists: Robin Congdon, 1 Ticklemore St, Totnes, TQ9 5EJ (01803 865926).

Recommended:
Robin Congdon, Beenleigh Blue: This cheese melts on the palate, disclosing its spicy, strong character.

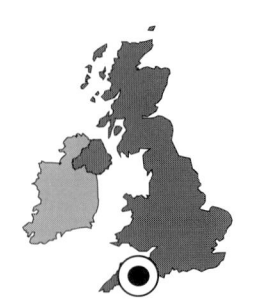

A vegetarian rennet is used to make this cheese, which makes it a popular choice as it can be eaten by all!

Berkswell

Berkswell cheese is hand made at 16th Century Ram Hall, situated on the edge of Berkswell village, from which the cheese takes its name. This is a modern, vegetarian farmhouse cheese. It is made with unpasteurised ewe's milk, which explains some of the complex and amazing flavours that this cheese produces. It is a hard cheese with a fat content of 48%.

Appearance:
This cheese has a flattened, round shape. The deep russet-red natural rind bears the intricate marks of the basket mould in which it is made. The rind is hard and ridged, almost crusty. It has a firm, ivory paste.

Nose:
The rind has an aroma of lanolin and damp wool, probably from the ewes that were milked to make it!

Taste:
This cheese is hard and chewy, almost granular in texture. The taste is very complex on the palate, with a combination of roasted nuts, caramelised onions and meadow flowers with a prickly tang making the old idea that all cheese tastes 'like cheese' quite unfounded. Others have described it as having

a 'silky' flavour, and we agree because it is quite full and rich, and yet sweet on the tongue. Fabulous flavour!

Overall opinion of cheese:
To be honest, none of us had never thought about eating a hard, unpasteurised ewe's milk cheese before, let alone enjoying it, but this close textured cheese is a must for a good cheese board. It is highly recommendable for anyone who is, like we were, a little afraid to try something a bit different.

Production: This cheese is made using the milk from a flock of 350 homebred Friesland ewes. The Friesland ewe has two important characteristics, which help make this cheese taste so different. Firstly, the high yield milk; this is a result of an ability to have large litters of lambs – as many as 5-6 each! Secondly, the ewe has a placid temperament. This may seem strange, but few breeds of sheep could cope with the twice-daily routine of machine milking and the constant human contact. We have been told that Friesland sheep are incredibly greedy and the opportunity to feed in the milking parlour is one not to be missed! The whole cheesemaking cycle begins with the birth of lambs. After giving birth the lactation will last for approximately 250 days. At Ram Hall the flock is divided into two groups, 200 ewes in January and the rest in late March. Their diet consists of a mixture of grass and maize silage and concentration feed is introduced 4 weeks prior to lambing. For the first 7 months of her lactation she is milked twice a day, and for the final 4-6 weeks this is reduced to once a day. The best ewes will give a total lactation of 450+ litres – as much as 4-5 litres a day!

This cheese was developed from a traditional Caerphilly recipe, but adapted and matured for 4-8 months to give it its unique texture and flavour.

Eating and drink: Berkswell is often recommended for grating as it is compared favourably with a mature Pecorino. It can also be enjoyed on a cheese board. Recommendations of wine include Cotes du Rhone – Parallele 45, Paul Jaboulet Aine and Qunita de la Rosa – Douro Red. These wines are both very rich and fruity in flavour.

Storage: This cheese should have a hard and crusty protective rind, which has an aroma of damp wool – if it doesn't then don't purchase!

Produced: This cheese is hand made at 16th Century Ram Hall, on the edge of Berkswell village from which the cheese takes its name. It is made from the milk of Friesland ewes.

Stockists: Stephen Fletcher, Ram Hall, Berkswell, Coventry, West Midlands, CV7 7BD (01676 532203).

Recommended:
Duddleswell: This is a modern, unpasteurised, vegetarian, hard cheese of truckle shape with hard, finally ridged, polished, natural rind. It was produced by Sussex High Weald Dairy. The cheese has a flaky texture with a sweet, caramel flavour along with a hint of Brazil nuts and fresh hay.

This cheese is named after the Saxon chief, Bercul, who was baptised in the ancient well at the centre of the village.

Bishop Kennedy

One of Scotland's finest cheeses, Bishop Kennedy was actually created by a young French cheesemaker, who was lured over to the Howgate cheesemakers in 1992. His mission was to invent a washed-rind cheese with Scottish attitude. After careful trials, he finally perfected a secret concoction, which included a generous amount of Scotch Whisky. The mixture is rubbed or smeared over the cheese during its maturation. These washings encourage the development of moulds, which produce a pungent flavour and aroma. The name Bishop Kennedy is taken from the 15th century Bishop of St. Andrews, who founded the famous St. Andrew's University, and whose niece is celebrated in the annual Kate Kennedy Pageant in the town.

Appearance:
The rind is red-orange coloured, and sticky to touch. The paste is a golden straw colour, and is very smooth and velvet in texture.

Nose:
Bishop Kennedy shares the typically pungent aroma of a washed rind cheese. The smell has been likened in the past to

damp washing, or old socks, but is described more politely as "yeasty".

Taste:
The flavour is very full, with heavy cream and yeast elements, and a long strong spicy finish.

Overall opinion of cheese:
A beautiful soft Scottish cheese, we feel that the cheesemaker has more than fulfilled his brief!

Production: Bishop Kennedy is produced using pasteurised cow's milk and rennet suitable for vegetarians. The maturing cheese is washed regularly during maturation to produce the strength of aroma and flavour. The cheese is made into wheels approximately 30cm in diameter and 2cm thick. It can also be obtained in miniature wheels of 10cm in diameter. These smaller versions are sometimes known as "Bishop's Bairns".

Eating and drink: Bishop Kennedy is best enjoyed with a full bodied red wine, possibly a good Shiraz, or a generous dram of single malt whisky.

Storage: Bishop Kennedy is often bought young and can be matured for up to eight weeks when stored correctly. This depends on the conditions, but the cheese should be allowed to breathe, though not to dry out. We would suggest storage in a fridge, loosely wrapped in a cloth or similar.

Produced: Kinfauns, Perthshire, Scotland.

Stockists: Howgate Farmhouse Cheesemakers,
Kinfauns Home Farm, Kinfauns,
Perth, Perthshire, PH2 7JZ (01738 443440).

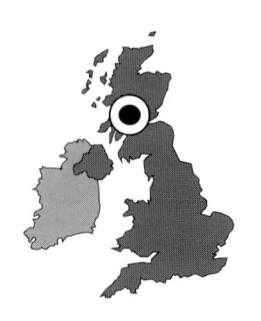

Scotland's smallest distillery produces the whisky especially for the washing of the rind to produce the unique flavour of Bishop Kennedy.

Cashel Blue

This is Ireland's most famous cheese and was also its first farmhouse blue cheese. It is made on the dairy farm of Jane and Louis Grubb near Cashel in County Tipperary. They began making Cashel Blue in the 1980's after spotting a niche in the market, and since then it has gained an enviable international reputation as one of the best cheeses to come out of the Emerald Isle.

Appearance:
Cashel Blue cheese has a cylindrical shape. It has a wet, crusty rind with grey moulds. The cheese is firm yet quite moist. It has an appearance similar to that of Docelatte.

Nose:
It has a nose of tarragon and white wine. It has an aroma that is similar to Roquefort, yet slightly ammonia.

Taste:
Cashel is a smooth, rich, full flavoured cheese, which is slightly spicy. It is less salty than most blue cheeses. It has a sharp tang that combines with the creamy richness to make a wonderful cheese.

Overall opinion of cheese:
We are supposed to be impartial in this book but we can't recommend this cheese enough. It is quite simply the best blue cheese any of us have ever tasted and many experts agree. Its melt in the mouth creaminess and rounded, mellow flavours are indescribable, and believe us, we are trying. Taste and enjoy!

Production: Cashel Blue is made from the milk of Jane and Louis' own herd of 110 Fresian cows. It is made in a similar way to Roquefort although it is softer, moister and less salty. The milk is pasteurised, cooled, inoculated with Penicillium Roquefortii and left at 32°C to allow acidity to rise. Cashel Blue used to be made using both pasteurised and unpasteurised milk but this has since changed. Rennet is then added, which causes the milk to coagulate, and the curd is cut with a cheese harp resulting in 'curds and whey'. The curd is then scooped out using scrim cloths (raw Irish linen), drained and tipped straight into the moulds. For the next few days it is left to drain with regular turning until it is dry enough for salting. There are many different processes involving the addition of salt, the one chosen for Cashel Blue being dry salting. This involves the rubbing of crystalline salt onto the surface of the cheese at intervals over two days. The cheese is then placed onto turntables and rotated whilst being pierced with long stainless steel needles in order to allow air into the cheese, thus creating the blue mould. The cheese is then transferred to cave-like conditions and the blue mould develops within two weeks. The mould is washed off the outside and the cheese is wrapped in gold foil. An appropriate colour for such a high standard of cheese!

Eating and drink: The cheese should be allowed to warm up to room temperature before serving on a cheese board. It is best served with plain unsalted biscuits such as water biscuits. We would recommend spreading it thickly onto a slice of warm walnut bread for the ultimate in dining experiences. Light fruity wines go well with Cashel Blue. Recommended wines include the 1996 red Chateau Lesalle from Bordeaux Superior, red and white Cote du Rhone, or a red Chateauneuf du Pape. Some people even like to find their Irish side and enjoy it with a glass of whisky! Cashel Blue goes very well with dark, strong beers such as Imperial Stouts, for example from Mt.Hood, Oregon's Full Sail Brewery Company (7% ABV). The sweetness of the ale coupled with the cheese's rich roastiness and slightly oily mouth feel is the perfect combination.

Storage: Storing the cheese in foil in a refrigerator or cool larder allows the cheese to slowly mature further until the required ripening is achieved. A full flavoured ripe Cashel is soft to handle whereas a young mild cheese is firm and crumbly.

Produced: This is the only blue cheese made by Jane and Louis Grubb. Each block of Cashel Blue carries a batch code number. The first two numbers correspond to the day of the week so that the age of the cheese is always known.

Stockists: J&L Grubb Ltd Farmhouse Cheesemaker, Beechmount, Fethard, Co Tipperary, Republic Of Ireland (052 31151).

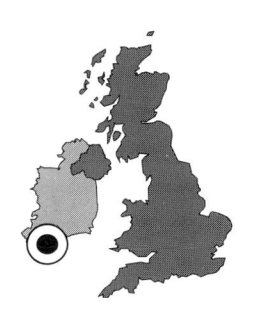

Recommended: There is nothing better!

The cheese takes its name from the Rock of Cashel, a bold outcrop overlooking the Tipperary plains.

Celtic Promise

This cheese was voted the Supreme Champion at the 1998 British Cheese Awards and has been described by Robert Morgan, Secretary of the Welsh Cheese Board, as being 'simply the best Welsh cheese, sorry, the best cheese from anywhere, available at the moment!' This is a modern, vegetarian farmhouse cheese. Celtic Promise is made with unpasteurised cow's milk. It is a semi-soft cheese with a fat content of 48%.

Appearance:
This cheese has a round shape, which is similar to that of a dumpling. The rind is smooth and orange in colour. Celtic Promise is a washed rind cheese with quite a moist centre. It has a creamy, rich yellow paste, which is soft to the touch.

Nose:
The rind is quite pungent. Many people are put off by the intense aroma which has been classed by experts as 'over powering' and even described by one as 'Pungent aroma is an understatement, never mind Celtic Promise how about Celtic Smell from Hell. Hideously smelly but if you like extreme sensory experiences, not to be missed.'

Taste:
Celtic Promise has a rich, creamy texture and a wide range of flavours, which is probably due to the complexity of the milk. By this we mean that the richness of the soil and the large variety of grasses, flowers and herbs that grow in the meadows and the surrounding hedges have a definite impact on the taste. The aroma doesn't carry through onto the palate, which is quite piquant yet delicate. The flavour is smooth, supple and even has a hint of spice.

Overall opinion of cheese:
Many people are put off by the aroma, but because of this, Celtic Promise is very much the choice of the connoisseur. This is one of the best cheeses from Wales, if not *the* best, and we recommend that, if you can overcome the smell, you will not be disappointed!

Production: James Aldridge has become renowned as a maturer and developer of 'real cheeses'. In the early 1980's he had a shop of his own, and used to collect the cheese from the farms himself. In order to save on transport costs, he would take as many as he could each time, and this naturally led to him finding ways of maturing cheese himself. He also inspires others to make real cheese and provides a service to budding cheesemakers, offering advice on techniques. This cheese is made from unpasteurised cow's milk and takes about 8 weeks to ripen. The technique used on the rind is called 'smear ripening' as opposed to rind washing, which is a description more correctly used to describe the preparation of French-style cheeses such as Epoisses. Celtic Promise begins life as Teifi cheese, made in West Wales. James Aldridge ripens the cheese in cider, which gives it the distinctive orange rind and fruity smell. The surface of the cheese is then washed or wiped by a cloth soaked in brine and containing a bacterium called Brevibacterium Linens, often with other selected micro-organisms, which gives the cheese its distinctive colour.

Eating and drink: Celtic Promise is a relatively new cheese so we are still experimenting as to what goes best with it. It is excellent as part of a cheese board and may be accompanied by cider. Some recommended wines are 1997 red Chateau Moulin Brule from Lussac St. Emillion and 1998 red Shiraz by Simon Hackett.

Storage: Robert Morgan informed us that the rind could range in colour from orange to terracotta and it has a dusting of moulds. The cheese should be loosely wrapped, and refrigerated, before being allowed to return to room temperature before service.

Produced: This cheese is a new cheese from the Teifi Farmhouse owned by John and Patrice Savage-Ontswedder.

Stockists: Teifi Farmhouse Cheese, Glynhynod, Llandysul, Ceredigon. (01239 851528).

Recommended:
Cwmtawe Pecorino: Round shaped, vegetarian, hard cheese introduced by Giovanni Irranca on his farm. This Pecorino-style cheese is renowned for its aromatic, vaguely almond aromas. When young, the cheese is creamy. It is used as a table cheese and for grating.

Celtic Promise has such a strong smell that someone once said that the taste is interesting 'once the nose has anaesthetised your sense of smell' !

Cheddar

Ah yes, Cheddar. Probably the most well known cheese in the world, thanks to its rich heritage and universal appeal. You'll no doubt be glad to hear that British Cheddar is acknowledged as being the best variety, though Canada and New Zealand have also managed to produce their own reasonable versions of it too.
Cheddar's history goes back hundreds of years, specifically to the 15th century when it was first made in Somerset and matured in the Caves that we know as Cheddar Gorge. Records show that it was also a particular favourite of King Henry II, who declared it to be the best cheese in Britain.
Fully cured, Cheddar falls into the 'semi-hard' cheese category, so you will find it has that wonderful suede texture when cut. It is traditionally made in a 'truckle', that is, a drum shape that has a hard natural rind, and is usually bound in cloth.
Age is the key factor to consider when purchasing Cheddar. A younger variety will have a smooth texture and mellow, creamy taste, having been matured for around six to nine months. Medium varieties undergo a slightly longer maturation process and have a similar flavour.
The real beauties however, and the ones we would recommend, are the mature and vintage types, which can be matured for anything up to 3 years. This ageing process allows the flavour to truly develop and brings out the strength and sharpness in its taste. When trying

cheeses of these types, look for the distinctive 'burn' in the mouth, and a lingering, nutty aftertaste. It is also quite common to detect a fruitiness such as apple or pineapple in the flavour and aroma.

Appearance:
Ranges from pale, almost white in colour, to buttery yellow. Some versions with colouring added can be as dark as Red Leicester.

Nose:
Often has a distinct fruitiness, and the more mature varieties have a characteristic 'barnyard' aroma. A slight earthiness is usually present due to the rind.

Taste:
Again slightly fruity towards the finish, younger ones tend to be more mellow whereas more mature versions can have a fierce 'burn' or tang. Cheddar is often creamy on the palate with a superb depth of flavour.

Overall opinion of cheese:
Undoubtedly one of the best, the flavour and aroma combined with its versatility makes Cheddar a firm favourite with virtually anyone with an eye for cheese. See our recommended types below that simply must be tried.

Production: Cheddar is one of the few cheeses around the world to be honoured with the *Protected Designation of Origin* status. This signifies that the West Country Farmhouse variety is only legally allowed to be made in the four counties of Somerset, Dorset, Devon and Cornwall.

Cheddar cheese is always made with full cream cow's milk. As with the majority of cheeses, it is much better if the milk is in its raw, or unpasteurised state. Firstly, the milk is heated to 86°F before the lactic starter culture is added. Rennet is added an hour later and the curd is allowed to firm. Once this has happened the curd is ground down into small pieces and heated again to 100°F. Following the discarding of the whey, it is sliced into slabs and pressed overnight. Having undergone the above process, the cheese begins its maturation journey, which as mentioned can be from nine months to as much as three years.

Eating and drink: Milder varieties of Cheddar pair extremely well with fresh apple juice, or for those wanting something a little stronger, a light white wine such as Zinfandel. Stronger versions are complemented perfectly with a good Merlot or a similarly fruity port. Strong dry cider also worked well for us, in addition to – wait for it – lager! (Try it if you don't believe us!)
We strongly believe that Cheddar belongs on any self-respecting person's cheese board, however its uses do stretch further. From a simple snack in a sandwich to the grated leftovers used in cooking, Cheddar is by nature a difficult cheese to waste. So don't do it!

Storage: This cheese can be far more forgiving than most others. It will sit out of a cool area for longer than you'd think, but of course we don't encourage this. When buying your cheddar whole, look for an undamaged rind with the distinctive mesh-like indentations from the cheesecloth, which indicate it underwent the traditional method of storage.
If buying your cheddar as a cut piece, check that it is moist enough to crumble slightly between the fingers but not leave an oily residue; this would imply that it has not been stored in cool enough conditions and has subsequently 'sweated'. Ensure also that it is not too dry – cracking is the most obvious sign of this – as you will end up with an inedible product. For more information on this topic, refer to the *Storage* section in the book.

Produced: With the exception of the West Country Farmhouse type, Cheddar is produced all over Britain in various forms. The Cheddar we highly recommend hails from the Quickes Dairy in Devon.

Stockists: Quickes Cheddar, Home Farm, Newton St Cyres, Exeter, Devon EX5 5AY (01392 851425).

Queen Victoria's wedding gift consisted of a giant truckle of Cheddar weighing in at over 1.000lbs!

Colston Bassett Stilton

This semi-hard blue cheese is known as the "king of cheeses" and is made using cow's milk. Stilton gets its name from the town where it was first introduced. Stilton, situated about 80 miles north of London, was, in the 18th century, a staging post for coaches travelling from London to York. Cooper Thornhill was the landlord at the famous Bell Inn and it was he who introduced the travellers to this soft, creamy, blue cheese. It was served with the top cut off and travellers allowed to spoon out the middle, although experts say that spooning out the middle ruins the flavour! Thornhill bought the cheese from a farmer's wife who lived near Melton Mowbray, and called it after the town where he lived. Despite this, Stilton cheese has never been made in Stilton!

Appearance:
This is a dry, well-formed cheese. It has a chalky grey rind, which is inedible.

Nose:
It smells young and mild. The rind has an aroma of a mushroom soup.

Taste:
The flavour is well developed with fruity hints and a smooth texture. It also has wine overtones.

Overall opinion of cheese:
This makes a great dessert cheese. It is also great for cooking with; we can recommend Stilton Mushrooms with freshly baked bread. A wonderful all-rounder, which can only be described as fabulous.

Production: Milk is pasteurised before it is used to make this cheese. Penicillium Roquefortii (which is what makes it blue) is added with starter cultures and milk clotting agents, such as rennet. Each cheese requires an amazing 24 pounds of salted curd which is fed into cylindrical moulds. After drainage these moulds are then placed on boards and turned daily to allow natural drainage for 5-6 days. If the turning process does not take place, then the cheese produced will be what we call 'Soggy Bottom', meaning that it takes the shape of a pyramid, with the top half being white and the blue having sunk to the bottom. As the cheese is never pressed, it creates a flaky, open texture required for the important bluing stage. After 5-6 days these cylinders are removed, and, to prevent any air entering inside the cheese, they are sealed by smoothing or wrapping. The traditional Stilton crust is formed after about 6 weeks. It is then ready for piercing with stainless steel needles. This creates the blue veins due to air being able to enter the body of the cheese. The cheese is ready to be sold after 9 weeks of age, by which time its weight should be a hefty 17 pounds, two-thirds its original weight. At this stage a plug of cheese is extracted and by visual inspection and smell it can be determined whether the cheese is up to the mark and able to be sold as Stilton. The cheese that does not meet these standards is then sold as blue cheese. Customers who prefer a more mature cheese would allow it to develop for a further 5-6 weeks, and it will then have a smoother, almost buttery texture with a rounded mellow flavour.

Eating and drink: We feel that this particular Stilton is so good that it can be eaten with anything at anytime! Traditionally though, Stilton is eaten at the end of the meal, or is often enjoyed with a pint of beer, as part of a Ploughman's Lunch. It also makes a good 'butter' for the top of your favourite steak or cutlets. Recommendations for wine include Coteaux du Languedoc - Domaine Sainte Sophie and Chateaux Panchille - Bordeaux Superieur; these are well-structured wines with full flavours, and complement this "king of cheeses" well!

Storage: Lisa from Silver Hill Dairy advised us that the crust of the Stilton should be perfectly formed and have no visible cracks; if this isn't the case, don't buy the cheese! The rind should be dry, rough, brown and most importantly, inedible! The interior should appear crumbly; yet moist enough to hold its shape, and be creamy and ivory in colour. Stilton, as with the majority of cheeses, should always be refrigerated until required. When needed, it should be removed and left to come to room temperature with the wrapping still loosely covering the surface of the cheese. It will keep for about six weeks if the wrapping is changed occasionally to avoid moisture build up. It can actually be frozen if not needed immediately, due to its strong robust flavours, which aren't lost during the freezing process, unlike many other cheeses. If you do choose to freeze it, it must firstly be wrapped in cling film, then aluminium foil and will keep in the freezer for up to a month. When defrosting Stilton it is important to put it into the fridge from the freezer for a 24-hour period, which prevents moisture loss and thereby retains the creaminess that Stilton is renowned for.

Produced: This cheese is produced in Nottinghamshire at the Colston Basset Dairy. It is one of a few British cheeses granted the status of being a protected designation origin by the European

Commission, meaning that only cheese produced in Derbyshire, Leicestershire, and Nottinghamshire may be called 'Stilton'!

Stockists: Colston Bassett & District Dairy Ltd., Herby Lane, Colston Bassett, Nottinghamshire, NG12 3FN (01949 81322).

Recommended:
Harringtons Stilton: Similar to the Colston Bassett but a slightly different texture. Rich, creamy and another fabulous cheese, no wonder Stilton is known as "the king of cheeses".

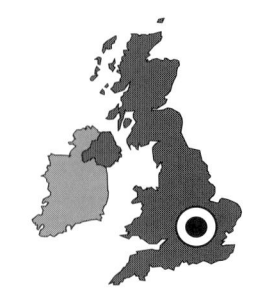

Traditionally Stilton was pierced with knitting needles and Port was encouraged to penetrate into the cheese - this is no longer deemed appropriate!

Cornish Brie

Brie is one of the most famous cheeses in the world. The original French version is known around the globe as the "queen of cheeses". We feel that the Cornish equivalent is an admirable cheese worthy of inclusion both in our guide, and in any cheese board selection.
The traditional Brie originated in the region of the same name, east of Paris. Its existence can be traced as far back as the eighth century.
It is said that Louis XVI requested one last taste of Brie before his arrest during the French revolution.
One of the most famous types of British Brie is St. Endellion, which is made with double cream and regarded as the ultimate in Cheese luxury.

Appearance:
A good Brie should be mature and soft, pliable and silky. The rind is soft and milky in colour, whereas the paste should be a deeper cream in colour. An immature Brie is characterised by a chalky residue under the rind, which, when left to develop further will become creamy and soft.

Nose:
The Brie nose is complex. There are notes of fresh cream, mixed with delicate elements of fungi, and cut grass.

Taste:
The creamy milk used gives this cheese a very rich, smooth flavour. The mushroom aromas follow into the taste and a heavy creamy finish can be enjoyed.

Overall opinion of cheese:
British Brie has always been regarded a poor cousin of its French ancestors, but we feel that this example proves that theory incorrect. Cornish Brie is another prime example of British cheesemaking standing shoulder to shoulder with the best in the world.

Production: Cornish Brie is made with unpasteurised cow's milk. A huge amount of milk (around 23 litres) is used to make each 3kg wheel. The milk is heated to 37°C during the renneting stage, but is never actually cooked. The cheese is then manually moulded using a pelle a Brie, or Brie shovel. Brie is then salted and maturation takes place in a cool cellar for a minimum of 4 weeks. The cheeses are gently turned several times during this period.

Eating and drink: Brie is an ideal cheese board soft cheese, and can also be enjoyed with warm bread, or cream crackers. We would recommend Shiraz as an ideal accompaniment to this cheese.

Storage: Although true for most cheese, it is essential that Brie is consumed at room temperature to enjoy it at its best. If possible, we would recommend retaining the original box for storage, otherwise loosely wrap in waxed paper or tin foil.

Produced: Newquay, Cornwall.

Stockists: Cornish Country Larder , The Creamery, Trevarrian, Newquay, Cornwall , TR8 4AH (01637 860331).

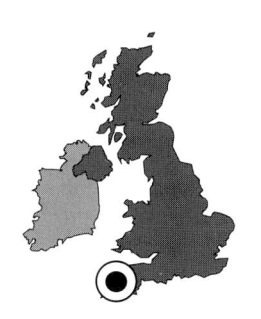

"Real" French Brie is one of the few un-stabilised cheeses left in the world; any Brie exported from France is stabilised for safety.

Cornish Yarg

This is a semi-hard cheese made from pasteurised cow's milk. The cheese dates back to the 17th century, and is these days produced using a vegetarian approved rennet substitute. The name of the cheese was derived from the maker's name, Gray – he wanted a Cornish sounding cheese so a friend suggested that he reversed his name from Gray, to Yarg! It is a moist cheese, which tastes fresh and creamy with a gentle tang. The cheese is coated in nettle leaves – traditionally this protected it from flies and stopped it from drying out too quickly.

Appearance:
It has an attractive rind that is greyish green in colour, due to the nettle leaves. The rind has green and white moulds that form in maturation. The white paste appears moist and crumbly.

Nose:
The rind has a musty, vegetal aroma, again due to the nettles and moulds. The paste has citrusy aromas with delicate lactic acid undertones.

Taste:
The cheese has a sharp acidic start with a great creamy finish. We recommend eating it with the rind, so that you get a whole marriage of flavours, like eating cheese and salad all in one. It has a smooth texture, creamy by the rind and slightly crumbly in the centre. The young cheese is fresh and lemony with a touch of herbs, while an older Yarg loses its lemon tang and develops a more aromatic and peppery flavour with vegetal undertones.

Overall opinion of cheese:
This cheese is great for any cheese board. It has a great look about it, a cheese with interest. It has been made with passion and this becomes obvious through the complex flavours it offers.

Production: The curds are cut by hand to release the whey when making this cheese. They are then milled, and left pressing overnight. They are placed in brine baths to be salted and coated in nettle leaves the next day. The nettle rind is edible, but many people discard it (not recommended!) The nettles are picked locally and frozen until required. They are dipped in sterilising solution and applied to the rind of the cheese using a brush. The cheese matures for anything from three to fifteen weeks in a ripening room.

Eating and drink: As mentioned, this is a superb cheese board cheese, or great with salads. A Rioja Rosado 1999 Rose wine makes a great accompaniment to Yarg or, if you prefer white wine, a Pinot Blanc, or even a good ale – all complement the complex flavours of this cheese.

Storage: Cornish Yarg should be stored at 5°C or below. The producers recommend storing in cheese paper or cling film and as always, remove it from the fridge one hour before use. Once the cheese has been cut it will store for a further 10 days.

Produced: This cheese was traditionally produced in Cornwall, at the Duchy of Cornwall Estate. The dairy has recently opened a visitor's centre, which has proved to be very popular.

Stockists: Lynher Dairies Cheese Company Limited, Netherton Farm, Upton Cross, Liskeard, Cornwall, PL14 5BD (01579 363128).

Freezing the nettle leaves removes the sting and causes the leaves to become limp and thus easier to apply to the rind of the cheese!

Derby

This hard cheese is made from pasteurised cow's milk. The Fowlers of Earlswood have been making Derby cheese since 1840, which, surely makes them eligible for the "oldest cheesemaking family in Britain" award! Originally, Derby cheese contained Annatto, the natural colouring used in many cheeses, but over the years this practice has stopped. Derby is described as a cheese that is very similar to Cheddar, although Derby has a softer, flakier curd with a buttery taste. During the war, Derby was one of the few British cheeses still allowed to be produced. It is described as an excellent alternative to 'real cheese' for pregnant women as it is made from pasteurised milk, but has all the taste of an unpasteurised cheese.

Appearance:
A Cheddar like appearance, butter looking with a natural orangey yellow rind.

Nose:
This cheese has a fresh aroma. There are strong creamy tones and a slight butternut hint.

Taste:
This cheese has a close texture that is flaky with a buttery finish.

Overall opinion of cheese:
This is a great alternative to Cheddar, with a medium flavour, and, like Cheddar, great for cooking.

Production: This cheese is pressed into cylinders and has a natural rind. Fowlers of Earlswood wash their rinds in red wine, which gives them an orange colour. It was the first cheese in the UK to be made in a factory, and some say that when they signed the contract, they signed the cheese's death warrant! Derby is often sold when it is immature, although at this stage, it lacks in flavour. It is at its best when left to age. It is matured for anything from one to six months.

Eating and drink: Derby can be used in cooking or deserves a place on any cheese board. The cheese is complemented by red wine, either Gamay de Touraine or Pinot Noir. It is a good cheese on its own or is great with a glass of beer.

Storage: As with any cheese, Derby should be stored in the fridge until required, then allowed to come to room temperature for at least an hour loosely covered by its wrapping. It should be stored in either cheese paper or cling film. It isn't recommended for freezing, but if using it for cooking, it can be stored frozen if grated and used straight from the freezer.

Produced: This cheese was traditionally produced in Derbyshire, but is now made in Warwickshire. The first cheese factory appeared in Derbyshire in the village of Longford in 1870.

Stockists: Fowlers Forest Dairy Ltd. Small Lane Earlswood, Solihull, B94 5EL (01564 702329).

Recommended:
Fowlers of Earlswood, Little Derby: This is probably the best Derby cheese available today.

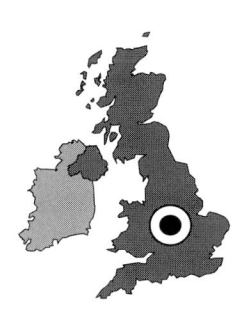

Traditionally the term 'little Derby' refers to Derby cheese produced outside of Derbyshire - this can be misleading as the cheeses weigh around 40kg!

Devon Blue

Devon Blue is another wonderful creation of Robin Congdon at the Ticklemore Cheese Company. Better known for his excellent goat and ewe's milk cheeses, Robin also makes this cow's milk cheese from the farm's own herd of Ayreshires.

Appearance:
Produced in a cylindrical mould, Devon Blue has a rough, crusty natural rind mottled with grey, white and brown moulds. The paste is yellow, stippled with blue, and is crumbly in texture.

Nose:
Mellow for a blue cheese, the aroma is very creamy, with only delicate blue notes.

Taste:
Mild and subtle, Devon blue is a very well balanced flavour, with hints of new leather, and strong herbaceous tones. The finish is strong with the sweet tang of any blue completing a wonderful flavour.

Overall opinion of cheese:
Devon Blue is undoubtedly a further testament to the skilful cheesemaking of Robin and his team. Its subtle nature belies a complex and rewarding blue cheese, without the overpowering tang associated with some English blues.

Production: Never one to follow tradition, Robin Congdon again surprises us with the production methods for Devon Blue. The cheese is made using unpasteurised cow's milk and vegetarian rennet. The milk is first warmed, before the starter is added. Penicillium Roquefortii is added to produce the mould. Unlike most cheese, the curds for Devon blue are moulded without draining; instead, the moulded cheeses are turned several times on the first day, and once on the second. After around 28 days, when a satisfactory mould has occurred, Robin wraps the cheeses in a gold foil. (This method is favoured by the French, rather than Stilton makers.) The cheeses are then matured for 6 to 8 months by which time the mould has developed fully. The finished cheeses are 3kg cylinders.

Eating and drink: Excellent on any cheese board, Devon blue is best enjoyed with a spicy wine such as Cotes du Rhone, or a good Rioja. It can also be served alone, with a nice big glass of Cider!

Storage: Devon Blue should be stored in the foil to prevent drying, and should be brought to room temperature before service.

Produced: Robin Congdon farms the Sharpham estate overlooking the Dart Estuary in Devon.

Stockists: Sharpham Creamery, Ashprington, Totnes, Devon, TQ9 7UT (01803 732600).

Robin Congdon produces a number of the cheeses featured in this book, and each one is very different. Try the lot!

Ducketts Caerphilly

Caerphilly is arguably the most famous of Welsh cheeses, and has been made since the 19th century. Caerphilly was developed in the surrounding farms of the small town of the same name. It became a popular choice for miners, and an instant hit throughout the country. It was already known that cheese absorbed some of the toxins inhaled during mining, and as such, many miners chose cheddar as a lunch. When Caerphilly became available, however, its fresher flavour and softer texture made it far more palatable for those men "down the pit". When the use of steam power became popular during the early 20th century, Welsh farmers and cheese producers found it more profitable to export their milk to English cheesemakers than produce Caerphilly themselves. The gap in production was filled by the Cheddar makers in the Bristol Channel. Because of the fast maturation period of the cheese (7-10 days), they found it more profitable to produce than Cheddar.
During World War 2, the production of Caerphilly, along with many other non-cheddar cheeses, was restricted to amounts needed for personal consumption. The cheesemakers of Wales were hit particularly hard by this legislation, and the industry took several decades to fully recover. It was during this recovery that Caerphilly began to be produced in bulk in Wales once more.

Our recommended Caerphilly is produced in Somerset. It is made to a family recipe three generations old.

Appearance:
Caerphilly is a moist, crumbly cheese, soft to touch. It is usually found in wheels, with a white rind dusted with very fine flour.

Nose:
A sharp but not overpowering milky nose, with surprising floral notes.

Taste:
Slightly sour, but strong butter flavours dominate this cheese, which is best enjoyed fresh, but can be matured to produce a more crumbly, complex flavour.

Overall opinion of cheese:
Although sometimes regarded as slightly bland and un-sophisticated, we feel that Caerphilly has an important place in British cheese history. We would include it on most conservative cheese boards.

Production: Caerphilly is made within a four-hour process, from unpasteurised milk and vegetarian rennet. The rind is formed by brining for 24 hours after pressing. The cheeses are then dried to harden the rind.
It is normally ready to eat within a week of production, although it can be matured for up to 10 weeks.

Eating and drink: Caerphilly can be rather bland when eaten alone, so we would recommend serving with fruit, particularly sweet apples or bananas. A good Pinot Gris would also be a lovely accompaniment.

Storage: Storage should not be a major concern with Caerphilly, as most people enjoy it when it is very young, but we would recommend refrigeration to retain the fresh flavours for as long as possible.

Produced: Wedmore, Somerset.

Stockists: Duckett R.E.G, Sexeys Farm, School Lane, Blackford Wedmore, Somerset, BS28 4NX (01934 712012).

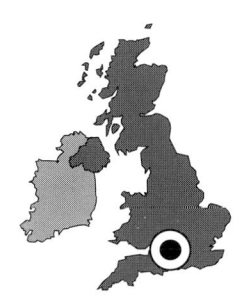

Ducketts produce their cheeses using traditional equipment, including an antique Victorian double cheese press.

Duddleswell

This is a modern, unpasteurised, hard cheese made from ewe's milk. Mark Hardy and his father make it in Sussex with the milk of the high weald dairy sheep, at the Putlands Farm in the Ashdown Forest. The cheese has become very popular and has won a silver medal at the British cheese awards and other awards internationally. Mark and his father have been producing cheese for over ten years now, and they make a range of ewe's milk products.

Appearance:
The appearance is flaky, yet firm. The curd is pale in the centre, and darker toward the rind.

Nose:
It smells sweet with fresh hay undertones.

Taste:
It has a distinct caramel flavour, and a nutty undertone, Brazil nuts perhaps?

Overall opinion of cheese:
This cheese deserves to appear on any cheese board. It has a smooth, creamy texture and acts as a great introduction to ewe's milk cheeses.

Production: Duddleswell is pressed into truckles around 4.5 lbs. in weight. The affinage period for this cheese is around ten to twelve weeks, and in this time a hard natural rind forms. This rind appears speckly and gives the cheese an attractive appearance. The cheese is made using a vegetarian approved rennet, which makes it a popular choice. As well as the plain variety, speciality versions are available, featuring chive and crushed pepper. Duddleswell is also available smoked.

Eating and drink: This cheese is recommended as a suitable substitute for Pecorino, which means it is a great cooking cheese or for grating. It can, as mentioned, appear on a cheese board. Eat this cheese with a soft red wine (one with no hard tannins – these exaggerate the salt), or a rosé; if you prefer white wine, choose a dry white.

Storage: The producers suggest that it should be kept in either the paper it is supplied in or wrapped in foil, and kept in a plastic box until required. It should, as with any cheese, be removed from the fridge an hour before serving, and lightly covered in the wrapping to allow it to breathe.

Produced: This cheese is produced at High Weald Dairy in Sussex by father and son team, Guy and Mark Hardy.

Stockists: Sussex High Weald Dairy Sheep Products, Putlands Farm, Duddleswell, Uckfield, East Sussex, TN22 3BJ (01825 712647).

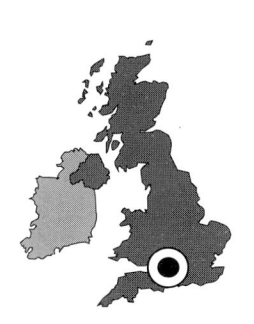

The Ashdown Forests have been the hunting grounds of English kings since 1372!

Durrus

This vegetarian, semi-soft cheese made from raw milk is very famous in the West Cork region and is produced in Jeffa Gill's dairy. Durrus matures in four to eight weeks and the fat content is 45%. Durrus is a washed rind cheese and was among the first in the new wave of Irish cheeses. Durrus breaks the mould. Two cheeses in one, Durrus starts life as a delicious and original 'new-age' Irish soft cheese and develops, with time, into a lovely, mouldy specimen with a stronger flavour. As golden, succulent and – when ripe – exquisitely smelly as a fine French semi-soft cheese, Durrus is in fact made in the far west of Europe, in Cork, on one of the many windy peninsulas that characterises that part of Ireland.

> **Appearance:**
> This cheese has a round shape with hard, smooth and dark brown natural rind, which has a hint of coral pink and ivory.
>
> **Nose:**
> There is the smell of the earth on the rind. The cheese gives off a sweet aroma, which follows on the palate.

Taste:
Whilst at Neals Yard we had the opportunity to taste a young and a mature piece of Durrus. The cheese when young is buttery, mild and slightly acidic and as such is compared to the French cheese Tomme. The cheese when fully mature gave off fabulous yet complex flavours. These included caramel toffee, tart apples and a hint of smoke, giving us a fairground or bonfire night feeling. The flavour of the Durrus is milky sweet with the texture oozy rather than runny. We even found it had a liquorice finish to it.

Overall opinion of cheese:
This is a pretty incredible, complex cheese full of strong flavours, which surrounds the palate. Durrus is similar to many washed rind cheeses but it has a definite sweetness that we weren't expecting. A remarkable offering from Jeffa Gill, the cheesemaker, whose background in fashion gives her "well rounded" cheese a little more character than one might expect from a larger company. Durrus has been described by many as being 'a subtle cheese, which is full of hidden secrets, sweet apples and pears, chocolate and even some say strawberries!'

Production: The cheese is made in rounds – a dinner-plate sized 3 lb. round or a little 12 oz disc. The surface of each cheese is washed several times in brine to encourage moistness and the growth of a bacterium known as Brevibacterium Linens, which gives a vaguely pink crust. This, in turn, causes the flavour of the cheese to develop – that is develop in a healthy, interesting way: it is a beneficial bug. The milk for Durrus comes from a neighbouring farm each morning and is processed in a magnificent, copper vat in Jeffa Gill's dairy. Over the next few weeks the natural moulds and yeasts in the air gradually form a coat, which both protects the cheese and helps in the ripening process. The high level of humidity on the west coast of

Ireland helps the bacterium work. The Brevibacterium Linens begin as a special, bought culture applied to the surface of the newly made cheese, but after a while it becomes established in the atmosphere of the maturing rooms of the dairy, too. It is due to the natural maturing that different people enjoy this fabulous cheese at different times. For example Jeffa Gill likes it at five or six weeks, when the flavour is deep but still mellow. A second stage of the crust, or rind, development is a fine furry grey mould – the French description 'cats' fur' is spot on – and this makes a stronger flavour. Neal's Yard boss Randolph Hodgson loves Durrus at this stage. Jeffa Gill says that if your whole Durrus is a bit fluffy it is fine to wipe the mould away – you can even rinse it under the tap then pat it dry!

Eating and drink: This cheese has such complex flavours that eating it with a water biscuit just won't do it justice. It is often eaten with, and is delicious on, a baguette accompanied with some fruit. Wine suggestions include soft, elegant Cabernet blends, such as a mature red Bordeaux or a subtler Californian. The subtle tones of Durrus are particularly well matched with a light Beaujolais Nouveau or an elegant Pinot Noir from Alsace. Durrus is good with salads or on its own. What does the creator herself Jeffa Gill like it with? 'It is a good cheese to go with fruit and I think pears are the nicest.'

Storage: Jeffa always keeps her cheese out of the fridge, on a board with a cover. Leaving it in the fridge is known to harm the ripening process too much.

Produced: Durrus is the name of Jeffa's village and Coomkeen, the name on the label, is her townland. Rural Ireland is divided into villages and townlands, a system that confusingly ends up with multiple families sharing the same address. Durrus itself boasts 26 townlands.

Stockists: Jeffa Gill, Coomkeen, Durrus, Bantry, Co. Cork (027 61100).

Recommended: St. Killian: Also from Ireland, this is an attractively boxed, Camembert style cheese, which has taken the market by storm. It has a strong mushroom aroma and a complex flavour, which combines butter with a bite of the grass that the cows have grazed on. This is produced by Patrick Berridge.

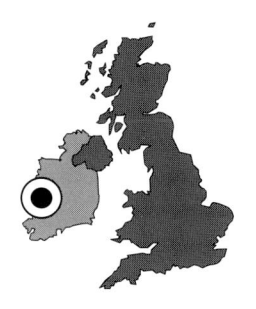

The sea breeze blasting in from the Atlantic must contribute some tang to the finished product, but cheese maker, Jeffa Gill, and her supporters at Neal's Yard Dairy, say that good milk and the cheese's crust are the decisive things.

Gubbeen Smoked

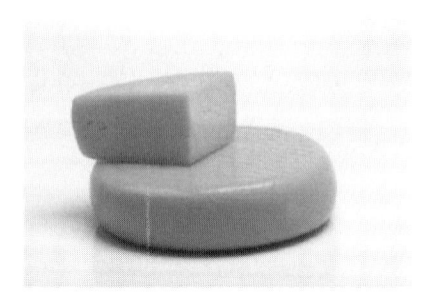

Gubbeen Smoked is named after Gubbeen house, the home of Giana and Tom Ferguson. It is found on the blunt peninsula to the west of Schull, Southwest Ireland. The Ferguson family have been farming there for five generations. Giana first learned of cheesemaking while at her uncle's house in France. After marrying Tom and settling down in Schull, she was inspired by the abundance of milk to attempt cheesemaking on her own. Her first attempts were produced in her kitchen, and were encouraged by Veronica Steele, maker of Milleens cheese. Twenty years later, Giana's cheesemaking continues, and has grown into a thriving business with an excellent reputation for quality cheeses.

Appearance:
The terracotta, brine washed rind has fine white and pale blue moulds, the paste is silky, buttery, and pliable in texture.

Nose:
Very smooth and creamy, oakey smells are produced by the smoking, which also produces the dominant notes on the nose.

Taste:
A creamy smoked flavour is dominant is this cheese, although the smoked flavour is beautifully balanced by careful preparation. A strong finish conjures up burnt onions.

Overall opinion of cheese:
An excellent table cheese, Gubbeen Smoked has twice won silver medals at the British Cheese Awards. We could find no reason why this success should not continue.

Production: Gubbeen is produced using the milk from Fresian, Guernsey, Simmenthal and the local, but rare black Kerry cattle. Following the example set by the majority of Irish cheesemakers, the cheese is now made with pasteurised milk. During the maturation process, the cheeses are regularly washed with a substance technically known as "goo". This is done to prevent the growth of bacteria normally encouraged in cheesemaking for fuller flavour. The cheeses are also turned regularly. Some of the cheeses are then oak-smoked to produce a light smoked flavour that the natural flavour of the cheese is still able to penetrate. The cheese is coated with thin yellow wax, and left to mature for three months.
Each finished cheese is 15cm in diameter and weighs 900g. Gubbeen is also available as a mini truckle weighing 400g.

Eating and drink: As a fairly traditional smoked cheese, Gubbeen is best enjoyed with bread or crackers. We found that the cheese was complemented by real ale or stout.

Storage: The wax rind provides adequate protection until opened, then the cheese should be loosely wrapped and refrigerated. Best enjoyed at room temperature.

Produced: Gubbeen House, Schull

Giana Ferguson, maker of Gubbeen smoked, is part Hungarian, and was brought up on a Spanish Mountain!

Hereford Hop

This traditional farmhouse speciality cheese is made using unpasteurised cow's milk. Hereford Hop is a soft cheese that is made in Gloucestershire by Charles Martell. Charles revived this old cheese in 1988. The cheese has an unusual rind of lightly toasted hops that is yellow to brown in colour. They are the same dried flowers that lend the bitter flavour to beers and ales, and are rubbed on the rind of the cheese according to medieval tradition.

Appearance:
The curd has a supple, Caerphilly like appearance, with a natural hop rind.

Nose:
The rind has a smell that one would associate with beers or ales. The curd has a mellow aroma.

Taste:
The rind has a slightly yeasty flavour, the curd has a silky smooth texture, the same as any good farmhouse cheese. The taste is sweet and buttery.

Overall opinion of cheese:
One of the great speciality cheeses, a unique experience with all the quality of a great British farmhouse cheese.

Production: Once pressed the cheeses are rubbed with lightly toasted hops and then matured. Whilst maturing the hops give the cheese a delicate, mild flavour with a strong yeasty aroma. It is produced using a vegetarian approved rennet and affinage takes from one to three months. It gets its name from the hops it is covered in, and as already mentioned, they also contribute greatly to the flavour.

Eating and drink: This cheese deserves to be eaten on its own! It has a unique flavour and appearance and is a great accompaniment to any cheese board. It should, of course, be enjoyed with a great British beer or ale.

Storage: This is the same as any cheese when it comes to storage. Store it in the fridge until required, and then allow it to come to room temperature for at least an hour. It should be stored in cling film or ideally in cheese paper.

Produced: This cheese is produced in Gloucester by Charles Martell at Laurel Farm. It is also produced by Malvern Cheesewrights, Malvern make a softer cheese that is matured for longer and has a stronger flavour.

Stockists: Laurel Farm, Dymock, Gloucestershire, GL18 2DP (01531 890637).

Recommended:
Charles Martell Hereford Hop: The traditional Hereford Hop made in Gloucester.

Malvern Cheesewrights Hereford Hop: This is a softer, stronger flavoured Hereford Hop produced in Worcester.

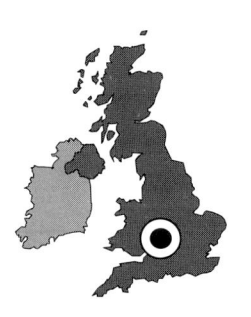

The rind is edible, but many people discard it - it has a yeasty flavour, people discard it due to its fairly bitter flavour!

Lanark Blue

This is a modern, farmhouse cheese made from unpasteurised ewe's milk. It is produced using a vegetarian approved rennet, and has won the silver medal at the British Cheese Awards in the past. The cheese is produced by Humphrey Errington, and it is thought he was the first person this century to produce ewe's milk cheese commercially in Scotland. His flock of sheep graze wild around 300 metres above the Clyde Valley, and along with Humphrey's expertise, the resulting cheese is sweet and aromatic. Humphrey read history at Cambridge, then worked abroad in the Far East, returned to Scotland in 1982 and began thinking about cheesemaking. In 1985 he produced his first Lanark Blue from his farm Walston Brahead at Ogcastle near Carnwath, with the help of Janet Galloway (an expert in Roquefort cheese) and her team. Lanark Blue is affected by seasonal change, and this is said to be due to the change in diet of the sheep: the cheese is medium flavoured in Spring, however in Winter, it takes on a very wild and full flavour. To keep cheese production flowing throughout the year, there are two flocks of sheep, one lambing in March and the other in October.

Appearance:
The rind is moist with grey and blue moulds. The paste appears mottled ivory white in colour with vivid green-blue moulds running through it.

Nose:
Its nose is that of a blue cheese, with salty undertones.

Taste:
This salty flavoured cheese is slightly sweet and pungent, very similar to Roquefort.

Overall opinion of cheese:
A great cheese with all the flavour and style of Roquefort.

Production: The cheese is handmade in the farm creamery. The Penicillium Roquefortii mould, which helps make the green-blue mould, is introduced to the unpasteurised milk at the start of the cheesemaking process. Once the curd has been formed into shape, (deep half moons) it is dipped twice in brine, and the cheese is never pressed. The cheese is then allowed to mature. After a month, the cheeses are wrapped in foil to avoid any further growth of surface mould, and allowed to continue to mature for a further two months. During this process they are turned three times a week. Once matured, they are scraped by hand and re-wrapped for sale.

Eating and drink: This is a fabulous cheese! A keen competitor to Roquefort, we should be proud it is produced in Great Britain. It deserves to be eaten on its own, but is great for cooking due to its strong, salty flavour. It should be eaten with a full-bodied red wine, a Shiraz or Cotes de Ventoux, for instance.

Storage: It should be stored in the fridge, with the foil it comes in providing appropriate wrapping, or alternatively using kitchen foil.

Lanark Blue doesn't have the same keeping qualities that we associate with its close competitor, Roquefort, and tends to turn brown with age.

Produced: This cheese is produced up in Lanarkshire by Humphrey Errington at his farm and creamery near Carnwath.

Stockists: Braehead Farm Walston, Ogscastle, Carnwath, ML11 8NF (0189 9810257).

Recommended: H J Errington & Co. Lanark Blue: This unique cheese is full of flavour.

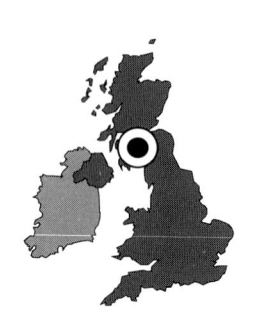

Some people find this cheese too salty – to solve this they mash it on their plate with unsalted butter - this is the same practice used by Roquefort eaters!

Lancashire

This hard cheese is made using cow's milk and has always been labelled a great cooking cheese. The cheese dates back many years and is mentioned in the Domesday book of 1086 – it is in fact one of the oldest cheeses still produced in Great Britain. The distinct character of the cheese originally derived from the salt marshes in which the cattle grazed, thus the cheese offers gentle green bitter tangs, with a salty finish. During the industrial revolution, Lancashire was the staple food of the mill workers and gets its name simply from the county where it was traditionally produced. Few of these cheeses are now produced in Lancashire and fewer still are produced on farms.

Appearance:
A young Lancashire will have a very white paste and will appear very crumbly; an older one would have a darker primrose paste and appear only slightly crumbly.

Nose:
The young cheese offers fresh, milky aromas; an older cheese has grassy and verdant aromas with leaf mould undertones.

Taste:
The young cheese has a soft, creamy texture that appears spreadable, moist and crumbly; it is sharp and has a distinct lemon tang. The older cheese again appears moist and crumbly; it has a smooth texture that is sharp and mellow with complex, grassy flavours and fruity undertones.

Overall opinion of cheese:
Lancashire is a powerful, good cooking cheese due to its strong flavours, a great toasting cheese!

Production: There are two types of Lancashire cheese, single curd and double curd. Double is more traditional and is so called because one batch of curds are made in the evening and left overnight; they are then added to fresh curds in the morning. Most of the Lancashire today is made from single curd, which gives it a drier, crumbly texture as compared to the double curds creamy and rich texture. Today there are still two producers who make the cheese from a combination of three days curds, which helps develop the flavours and textures and together they make for an unmissable treat. A young Lancashire is often referred to as 'creamy Lancashire', due to its smooth spreadable texture, and older Lancashire is known as 'tasty Lancashire' due to its sharp complex flavours. The cheese is pressed in to cylinders that can weigh anything from 9lbs – 40lbs and is then wrapped in cloth, which is necessary to keep it together at this stage. The cloth affects the flavour and texture of the cheese, allowing the cheese to lose moisture, and the flavour that is associated with the rind of the cheese is allowed to penetrate the cheese. Today they are also dipped in wax to prevent further moisture loss. A young cheese is matured for 3–6 months and an old one for no less then 9 months, which makes for a fine, strong tasting cheese.

Eating and drink: Lancashire, as mentioned, is a superb cooking cheese – how many times have you made a cheese sauce and then been disappointed because you can't taste the cheese? When using Lancashire you don't have this problem, as the flavours are so strong nothing can compete! It is also a great melting cheese and was traditionally known as the 'Leigh Toaster' after a small town near Manchester where it was produced; it melts into a sumptuous, velvety mass under the grill and thus makes amazing cheese on toast. Some people say that Lancashire cheese is best enjoyed with a glass of cola, the snobs say it is best enjoyed with either a Sauvignon Blanc or ruby port – the choice is yours!

Storage: Lancashire cheese should have a perfectly formed, hard thin natural rind that is pale gold in colour and have some blue, grey mould. A traditional cylinder will still bear the marks of the cloth. The interior should appear, according to its age, moist and crumbly. It must be stored in the fridge until required and removed around an hour before serving and allowed to come to room temperature with the wrapping loosely covering it to prevent it from drying out. Freezing is not recommended but Lancashire will keep for up to five weeks in the fridge. It is better to buy cheese as you eat it, as opposed to buying it in big blocks.

Produced: This cheese was traditionally produced in Lancashire and the first factory produced cheese appeared in 1913. Most of today's Lancashire cheese is produced at small creameries throughout Britain.

Stockists: Neal's Yard Dairy, 17, Shorts Gardens, London WC2H 9AT (0207 2405700).

Recommended:
Grandma Singletons: This cheese is a serious fully matured Lancashire with really strong flavours; it

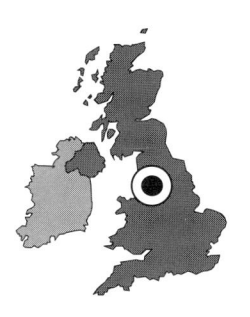

is covered in distinct red wax.

Shorrocks: This is still farm made and produced using unpasteurised milk; it has strong flavours.

Mrs Kirkmans: This is a multi award winning cheese. It is matured for five months and has a fantastic well-rounded flavour.

Sandhams: This Lancashire is organic and falls into the 'tasty' group of Lancashire cheese.

In days gone by, the hard rind of Lancashire cheese was given to babies to 'teethe on'.

Leicester

Another fiercely traditional British cheese, it is the main survivor of a range of cheeses that were made in the Midlands. This is a hard cheese and perhaps the most identifiable due to its reddish colour. The colour was traditionally achieved by adding carrot or beetroot juice to the milk. These days, however; this practice has been replaced by adding annatto (a colouring found in the seed pods of the tropical plant Bexa Orellana). It is often referred to as Red Leicester today, because in the Second World War all cheese producers were ordered to make 'National Cheese', and the practice of adding annatto to Leicester was banned. When the pale colour eventually returned to this cheese it became known as Red Leicester to distinguish it from the tasteless 'National Cheese'.

Appearance:
There should be an even colouring throughout the cheese, with a thin white powdery mould on the rind. It has a visibly cracked texture.

Nose:
It has a sweet aroma, like honey, with milky, bakery undertones. Smells like freshly cooked doughnuts.

Taste:
It has a crumbly, flaky texture. It is chewy and claggy and has a close consistency. The flavour of the cheese is mild with dairy undertones, a light burn and a granular finish.

Overall opinion of cheese:
This is a mellow, uncomplicated cheese that would be great for grilling, the table wine of cheese.

Production: The annatto colouring is added to the milk at the start of the process. Once the curds are formed they are pressed into moulds and wrapped in cloth, although a Leicester can be eaten young, it is recommended to allow it to mature for six to nine months, which helps develop the mellow flavours.

Eating and drink: This is another good cooking cheese, its reddish hue offering colour to cheese sauces and other cheese dishes. It can be enjoyed with a Rioja or Australian Shiraz, and is very good with a chilled ale.

Storage: There are no special requirements for the storage of this cheese – just follow the basic rule of keeping it refrigerated until use, and allow it to come to room temperature for at least an hour, loosely covered by its wrapping. It is not recommended to freeze the cheese, but if you are using it to cook with, you can freeze it grated, and use it straight from the freezer. A good Leicester should have an even reddish colouring all the way through with a fine, white, powdery mould on the rind.

Produced: This cheese was originally produced in the area surrounding Melton Mowbray (also famous for its pork pies). It was first produced commercially in around 1875.

Stockists: Times Past Cheese Dairy, Westfield Lane, Draycott, Cheddar, Somerset, England, BS27 3TP.

Recommended:
Times Gone Past Dairy Leicester: This is one of the few Leicester's made with unpasteurised milk and it makes all the difference!

Quickes: This is one of the more traditionally produced Red Leicester's with delicate flavours that improve with keeping!

Annatto was originally only used to colour the cheese, but it does in fact, contribute to the distinctive flavours that Leicester is famous for!

Milleens

This is one of the most exciting washed-rind cheeses to come out of Ireland in the last few years. It is made by Norman and Veronica Stale on their farm in West Cork. It matures in four to ten weeks and has a fat content of 45%. It was supreme champion at the 1997 British cheese Awards. Milleens is made on the Beara Peninsula in West Cork. This is a sharp, tangy and creamy washed rind cheese, and is made with a vegetarian rennet and raw milk.

Appearance:
Milleens is a semi soft farmhouse cheese with pinkish orange, brine washed, uneven, wrinkled rind. It has even been said that this cheese looks like a mildewed bulbous hockey puck!

Nose:
Its aroma is barnyardy with wet rocks and heather. To say that it has a strong aroma would be a slight understatement!

Taste:
This cheese has a rich, sweet flavour. It is spicy and very piquant in taste and aroma. Milleens is also quite a supple, sweet cheese, which we think also has hints of cream and butterscotch. At its peak its paste is known to become almost

fluid, and the taste is yeasty and savoury, with a strong, herbaceous tang and the suggestion of sea breezes.

Overall opinion of cheese:
Milleens has the sweet-sour taste associated with genuine Trappist cheeses. Like the famous Belgium beers, which were made by the Trappist monks, this to is an experience in itself.

Production: The milk comes from the farm's own cows and those of two neighbours, and the cattle graze the lower mountain slopes of Mishkirk Mountain, overlooking the Atlantic. After maturing on the farm for 2 or 3 weeks, the curd is scooped into moulds and left to drain. The high moisture of the curd and the humid maturation conditions produce a grey, hairy mould. Affinage can last up to six months. The rind is washed in a slightly salted brine. This is similar to most other semi-soft cheeses as it is rubbed, brushed, or washed with a liquid while curing. The liquid can be brine, whey, wine or spirits, and it fuels the growth of surface bacteria that affect the flavour of the cheeses. Milleens cheese is usually cured for longer periods than bloomy-rind cheeses and some develop thick crusts and others have sticky surfaces that encourage the development of the *linens* bacteria, which causes them to become very pungent and powerful in aroma. Despite the fact that they are so stinky, they vary in taste, some having very strong and pronounced flavours, while others are surprisingly mild. During maturation the cheeses are regularly washed to prevent the growth of Brevibacterium Linens (a bacteria encouraged in many cheeses since it produces lively flavours and aromas) with a substance known as 'goo'. The cheeses are also regularly turned as with the Stiltons.

Eating and drink: Serve this exciting cheese on its own, on a salad with chilled asparagus spears or slathered on some soda bread with a glass of stout to wash it down. Norman Steele suggests 'Milleens

likes to be with good bread (especially a brown Irish soda bread) and a glass or two of wine – certainly a decent burgundy or claret, or maybe a Barolo or Barbera from the Piedmont.'
Personally we think that eating Milleens with a bottle of Chimay, one of the best Belgian bottled beers available, would be an experience in itself.

Storage: Try Milleens whenever you can, as it changes with the seasons: summer cheeses being floral and fragrant; winter ones having a more salty, savoury taste. After tasting cheese from both times of the year we found that you can always rely on Milleens to be soft, yielding, rich and even romantic and comforting.
According to the creator Norman Steele 'Milleens cheese should be kept wrapped in a larder or fridge and then allowed to reach room temperature. After that, the best thing to do is to eat it. A restaurateur once took away from the house a small ripe Milleens (called a 'dote') and asked me how long it would last. It being a beautiful spring lunchtime, perfect for a picnic, I replied that if it lasted longer than the time taken to drive along the beautiful Kenmare river, he didn't deserve to have it.'

Produced: Veronica and Norman Steele had been making Milleens on the Beara Peninsula for more than 10 years, and it is seldom the same twice, though never disappointing.

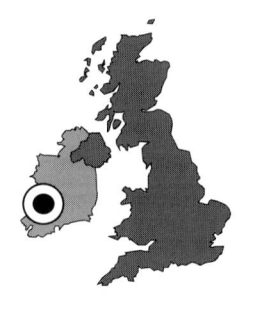

Stockists: Veronica and Norman Steele, Milleens, Eyeries, Beara, County Cork (027 74079).

The development of many of these cheeses can be traced back to monastic orders during the Middle Ages; therefore they are sometimes referred to as monastery cheeses.

Olde Gloster

British farmers have been experiencing difficulty for a number of years. Many have been forced to diversify or go out of business. One family facing such a dilemma was the Rogers family in the early 1990's. They decided, thankfully for cheese lovers, to move into cheesemaking with their 50 strong herd of Fresian dairy cattle.
The Rogers' farm is situated near Worcester, and produces Olde Gloster cheese, a variation on traditional double Gloucester cheese. Their facility has been built inside an old cart shed dating back over a century. The cheesemaking is a family business, with the responsibility of actually creating the cheese left to the son, Phillip Rogers.

Appearance:
A firm and moist texture with very rich orange paste.

Nose:
We were struck by the intense cream apparent in this cheese, although there is also a nutty quality about this nose.

Taste:
Olde Gloster has a sophisticated mellow flavour, although our tasters likened some samples to cheese and onion crisps!

There are definitely some strong vegetable flavours and the fruity, zesty finish is a delight.

Overall opinion of cheese:
The Rogers' endeavours have been justly rewarded here with a very exciting addition to the repertoire of British cheeses. Similar to Double Gloucester, yet somehow far more sophisticated, we would recommend that everyone try this cheese at least once!

Production: Olde Gloster is made using unpasteurised cow's milk and is hard pressed to produce a firm, close texture. The vibrant orange colouring comes from the addition of carrot juice into the milk. The cheeses are then left to mature for four to five months to allow the mellow flavour to develop.

Eating and drink: It seems almost a shame to put such an excellent cheese with anything but a small glass of water, but Olde Gloster is excellent as part of a traditional cheese board, or enjoyed singularly with a large glass of scrumpy cider. For those after a subtler beverage, we would recommend a good quality Beaujolais.

Storage: A very robust cheese, Olde Gloster is best loosely wrapped, and served at room temperature or below.

Stockists: Lightwood Cheese, Lower Lightwood Farm,
Lightwood Lane, Cotheridge, Worcester,
Worcestershire WR6 5LT
(01905 333468).

Produced: This cheese is produced on the Rogers' Farm near Worcester.

The Rogers family perform all the tasks associated with a large dairy virtually by themselves. These include bookkeeping, milking and running a small farm shop.

Sharphams

This is a soft, surface ripened cheese made from unpasteurised Jersey cow's milk at Sharpham Estate near Totnes in Devon.

Appearance:
This cheese has a golden curd and a mottled mushroom skin effect on the white bloom. It is chalky yet Brie like.

Nose:
It has a buttery nose. The rind smells like a rich mushroom soup. It has a delicate aroma.

Taste:
It has a creamy, complex trail of tastes, earthy yet sharp, smooth and yet mushroomy with a good long finish. The contrast between the centre of the cheese and the rind is amazing. It is almost like eating two different cheeses! The rind is earthy with the smooth part of the cheese almost melting in your mouth.

Overall Opinion:
This cheese has a unique flavour and creamy texture. This is a serious alternative to unpasteurised Brie du meaux – mind out

the French!

Production: The Jersey cattle enjoy extended grazing in the lush pastures above the meandering River Dart. The dairy undertook a two-year conversion programme resulting in them being awarded organic status for their herd from May 2001. Cheese-maker Debbie Mumford and her team currently hand produce three styles of unpasteurised cheeses with the rich creamy milk; two are soft and one semi hard. Sharphams is a coulommiers type cheese which has been hand made in the creamery to their own recipes since 1980. Salt, starter cultures and vegetarian rennet are the only additions to fresh Jersey milk. The curds are all hand ladled very gently into the moulds. This cheese definitely has the personal touch and this is proved in the taste! Debbie says "The cheese is turned and moulded when it is ready, not when the schedule says it should be."

Eating and drink: After speaking with Debbie we realised that many cheeses don't have specific foods that complement them well. We found that the same theory used with the selection of wines and food should be carried over to cheese and accompanying food. A strong cheese should be paired with a strong food, something that can stand up and won't lose its flavour. But we all agreed that a piece of just matured Sharphams is not bettered than when on a freshly baked French loaf. Wines from the estate of Sharphams complement the cheese very well.

Storage: It is important to buy this cheese just before it is ripe. The cheese should have a defined line of chalk running through the centre (similar to Brie but larger!). The rind should be white and bloomy. The cheese just to the inside of the rind should be pale yellow and soft to touch when ripe. Debbie states "when handling a cut piece of Sharphams, it should be kept in a fridge in cling film or in a plastic container. It is a bit of a myth nowadays that a cut piece can ripen because only a whole cheese can ripen in time".

Stockists: Sharpham Estate, Ashprington, Totnes, Devon. TQ9 7UT. (01803 732203).

Produced: Since the 18th Century the coachyard of Sharpham House has been the home of the Creamery. Sharpham took a further two Gold Medals at the British Cheese Awards in 2000, adding to an ever-growing list of accolades.

Recommended:
Sharpham's Elmhirst: This Elmhirst is a triple cream, mould ripened similar to a 'Vignotte'. It has a surprisingly light texture and delicate flavour if eaten young (2-3 weeks) but if matured for 4-6 weeks it becomes more rich and full bodied. Elmhirst is available in 1kg rounds or 250g squares.

Sharpham's Rustic: Available in plain or chive and garlic, the 'Rustic' is a semi-hard cheese which they mature for approximately 6-8 weeks, giving a youthful cheese with a moist, creamy texture. A thin natural rind forms during the maturation process. Available in 2kg rounds.

It is wrapped in paper with little holes so that it can ripen without becoming moist.

Swaledale

The Origin of Swaledale Cheese is uncertain, but popular belief is that the Christian Monks who arrived from Normandy first made it as far back as the 11th Century. This Swaledale cheese has the PDO (Protected Designation of Origin) and has been made in the Dales for more than 500 years. It is made using 100% ewe's milk giving it a little more body than the cow's version.

Appearance:
It has a white paste and develops a fine grey moulded rind.

Nose:
It has the freshness of the misty Yorkshire Dales and is mild on the nose. The rind carries a strong mushroom aroma.

Taste:
Light, creamy, moist texture and the fresh tang of Swaledale Cheese. It has a taste of wild bracken, along with the typical acidity associated with Dales cheeses.

Overall opinion of cheese:
This cheese is similar to Wensleydale with a softer and perhaps more lemony flavour. It becomes drier and fuller-flavoured with age.

Production: This Swaledale is hand-made with dedication by David and Mandy Reed in the historic town of Richmond, the gateway to Swaledale. It is made using vegetarian rennet. Their farm animals graze on the Upland slopes of the Yorkshire Dales National Park in an area which is designated as 'environmentally sensitive' and where farmers are discouraged from using artificial fertilisers. The cheeses are all made in the purpose built dairy combining the traditional recipe with today's stringent hygiene standards. Before it is left to mature in humid cellars, the cheese is soaked in brine that prevents it from drying out. The cheese matures for one month. During the 19th century, the ewe's milk Swaledale was sometimes kept for 3 to 4 years, becoming extremely pungent. Swaledale can be made throughout the year but is at its best when made in late spring.

Eating and drink: Recommended wines include the Reserve Merlot from Montes Curico Valley 1998/99 and the Old Vine Garnacha from Bodegas Guelbenza, Navarra, a red wine from 1996. David from the Swaledale Cheese Company suggested a water biscuit to match with the cheese as well as fresh fruit such as grapes, apples and even pears (these were his particular favourite!).

Storage: He also suggested that this cheese once cut should be covered in cling film or foil and left in the fridge.

Produced: The Swaledale Cheese Company in Yorkshire.

Stockists: The Swaledale Cheese Company, Mercury Road, Richmond, North Yorkshire DL10 4TQ (01748 824932).

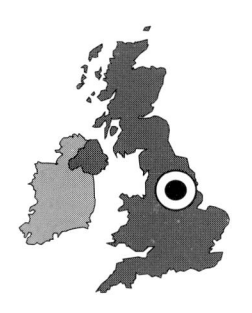

Recommended:
Lindisfarne Mead Cheese: this is a legend and 'the World's finest Mead'. It is only produced at St. Aidens Winery on Holy Island, using fermented white wine and the finest honey from around the world. The result is a mild creamy cheese with a sweet honey flavour.

The first Swaledales were blue cheeses and there are also variations of the ewe's milk version with fresh chives, garlic and apple and mint.

Ticklemore

Ticklemore cheese is made by Robin Congdon, of the Ticklemore Cheese Company, who has been farming the Sharpham Estate, overlooking the Dart Estuary, for nearly thirty years. The Cheese began its evolution with Robin's fascination with the microbes involved in cheesemaking. He began to make yoghurt with some of the milk produced by his ewes, and it was not long before he moved on to cheese. Robin has since become an expert in the cheesemaking microbes, which are critical to every aspect of producing a great cheese. Robin is a master of the unconventional, and Ticklemore is one of only a handful of hard goat's cheeses available.

Appearance:
Ticklemore is produced in an unusual flattened spherical form. The marks of the basket used to mould the cheese can be clearly seen on the rind of the finished product.

Nose:
Ticklemore is unconventional goat's cheese in as much as the overpowering aroma usually associated with such cheeses is not present. The delicate creamy aroma is very surprising for a hard cheese.

Taste:
The key word to remember when tasting Ticklemore is "delicate". Every aspect of the fairly complex flavours of this cheese is delicate to the point that you feel they will disappear if you chew too aggressively!

Overall opinion of cheese:
The unusual nature of Ticklemore hard goat's cheese makes it a must for the serious taster, but on a more practical level, it makes an ideal alternative hard cheese for those suffering from allergies to cow's milk.

Production: Ticklemore is produced using full fat, unpasteurised goat's milk. This means that the finished cheese has a relatively high fat content of 48%. The cheeses are then hand moulded in baskets, producing the unusual shape. The maturing period is between two and three months, and the cheeses are turned twice a week during this time.

Eating and drink: Ticklemore is very good on a cheese board, but really proves its worth when used in cooking, especially sweet dishes such as cheesecake. When eaten alone, it should be accompanied with a strong full flavoured fruity wine such as a good Brouilly.

Storage: Like most cheeses, Ticklemore can be stored loosely wrapped in the fridge, but is best enjoyed at room temperature.

Produced: Robin Congdon farms the Sharpham estate overlooking the Dart Estuary in Devon.

Stockists: Sharpham Creamery, Ashprington, Totnes Devon TQ9 7UT (01803 732600).

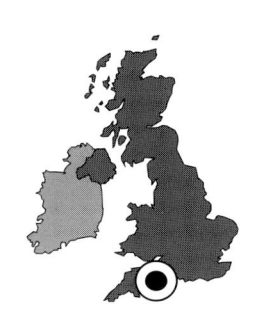

Ticklemore is one of the few remaining British Cheeses still hand moulded, giving it it's unique shape and "farmhouse texture".

Tymsboro

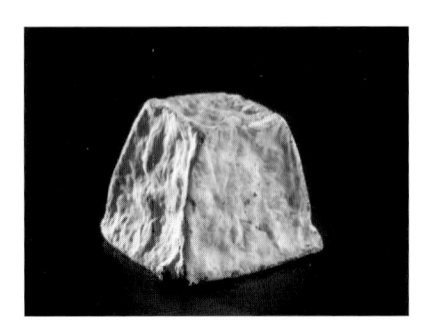

This is a vegetarian cheese made from unpasteurised goats milk. This soft cheese is produced by Mary Holbrook in Avon. Mary herself had never dreamt of farming, let alone cheesemaking, until her husband inherited the family farm in Somerset. When they moved in, Mary bought two goats as pets and in 1976 they moved to Sleight Farm, a beautiful building dating back to the 1820's. It is situated six hundred feet up in the Mendip Hills. Mary took the two goats with her and they were kidded down. She found they produced lots of milk, and this is when she turned her hand to cheesemaking. Tymsboro has won an award at the British Cheese Awards for the best soft white cheese.

Appearance:
This cheese is pressed into flat-topped pyramids. The natural rind is dusted with black ash and covered in a white bloom.

Nose:
The rind has a typical mushroomy aroma, the curd has fresh creamy tones.

Taste:
The taste can simply be described as lemony with a hint of apples.

Overall opinion of cheese:
This cheese is delicate, fresh and moist when young, and drier, more pungent and stronger when mature.

Production: The problem with goats is that they produce the least amount of milk in the winter, which is, unfortunately, when goat's cheese is most popular! Some farmers have got round this by dividing the herd into three. One third are mated at the start of the season, producing young in early Spring; the second third are mated at the end of the season producing kids in late Spring; and the final third have lighting installed in their shelters so that they are fooled into thinking they are enjoying the light nights of Summer. This means that as the light is turned off earlier and earlier the goat thinks it is entering Autumn and comes into season, thus they produce kids in late Summer – clever! The curds in this case are pressed into moulds and when settled the rind is rubbed with black ash. During the maturation period a natural white bloom grows on the cheese, affinage in this case taking two to four weeks. The cheeses are sometimes seasonal and available in the shops when they are in season.

Eating and drink: As an award winning cheese this cheese is wonderful by itself. It is one of the more interesting goat's cheeses available on the market today. Serve with an assertive white wine such as Pouilly, or Sancerre.

Storage: No special instructions here. It is best stored in the paper it is supplied in or alternatively foil or cling film. It is important to store it either in the fridge or somewhere else cool, such as the garage or shed. When required allow the cheese to come to room temperature, loosely covered by the wrapping.

Produced: This goat's cheese is produced in Avon by Mary Holbrook, and is at times a seasonal cheese.

Stockists: Mary Holbrook, Sleight Farm, Timsbury, Bath, BA3 1HN (01761 470620).

Mary also produced the popular hard goats cheese Mendip - the bad news is she doesn't make it any more; the good news is, it is going to be replaced by Tilleys – watch this space!

Waterloo

This semi-soft cheese produced from Guernsey cow's milk is made by Anne and Andy Wigmore in Berkshire. It is a washed curd cheese and has a golden curd that is typical of Guernsey milk cheeses. It has a thick, natural pinkish rind that is dusted with white moulds, and as it ages it becomes very grey, crusty and wrinkled. Waterloo is a very popular cheese here in Britain and has, in the past, won a silver medal at the British Cheese Awards. After Anne Wigmore spent ten years in dairy research at Reading University, conducting experiments with cheesemaking, she was fascinated and started producing cheese for home consumption, but it wasn't long before the bug set in, and she was addicted. Her husband joined her and today they produce three kinds of cheeses, including a ewe's milk cheese, Wigmore, and of course, Waterloo.

Appearance:
The rind looks off white in colour with browny moulds on it, the curd is deep yellow and looks very creamy and buttery.

Nose:
The rind gives off musty, mushroomy aromas, and the curd smells buttery.

Taste:
A young cheese is fruity and mellow, an older cheese takes on peppery flavours. A young cheese is firm but with time the proteins and fats break down making it almost runny.

Overall opinion of cheese:
An individual cheese with a golden curd that offers earthy flavours, it is often firm in the centre and creamier toward the rind.

Production: As mentioned the curds are washed before being pressed in moulds. The fat content of the cheese is 45%, which is due to the Guernsey cow's milk, typical for producing golden curds. They are allowed to mature for anything from four to ten weeks, depending at what age and state the cheese is required. Some prefer the young fruity cheese, whereas others like the peppery bite that is associated with an older cheese.

Eating and drink: The earthy flavours of this cheese make it a great cheese to appear on any cheese board. It is best eaten on a simple cracker and served with a white wine such as an un-oaked Chardonnay.

Storage: There are no special instructions when it comes to storing this cheese. Store it in the fridge wrapped in the paper it came in. It should be firm in the centre, and creamier towards the rind if not runny! Allow it to come to room temperature before consuming, as this allows the curds to fully ripen, and helps develop the flavours and soften the paste.

Produced: This cheese is produced in Berkshire by Anne and Andy Wigmore in the converted dairy next to their house.

Stockists: The Cottage, Basingstoke Road, Riseley, Reading, RG7 1QD (01189 884564).

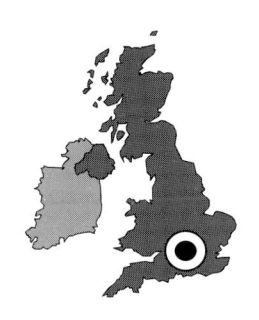

Anne and Andy manage to produce an amazing 1000 pounds of cheese a week. With only them and two part time workers this is quite an achievement!

Shepherd's Purse Wensleydale

It is believed that the first Wensleydale cheese was made by French monks who moved to Wensleydale in the 12th century. These monks were experienced cheesemakers, who sought advice from their cheesemaking colleagues in Roquefort, thus virtually ensuring the success of their creation. During the 14th century, cow's milk began to be used instead of ewe's, and this obviously affected the character of the cheese. At that time, Wensleydale was almost exclusively a blue cheese, so a little ewe's milk was still used to encourage the cultivation of the appropriate bacteria. In modern times, Blue Wensleydale is rare, with the vast majority of cheese taking the form of the more familiar, crumbly table cheese.

When the monastery closed in 1540, the local farms took over production, and this localised industry remained right up until the Second World War.

During the war, most of the milk production was required for "national cheese", and so Wensleydale became very rare. Indeed, even when rationing was stopped in 1954, the level of Wensleydale making, such as other British cheeses, failed to reach those seen before the war.

Wensleydale cheese experienced difficulty in recent years, and owes a great deal, possibly its entire survival to Nick Park's Oscar winning animations "Wallace and Gromit", in which this particular cheese is championed.

Appearance:
Shepherd's Purse Wensleydale has an open, and crumbly texture and is moist to touch. The cream wax rind envelops the cheese and protects the delicate paste.

Nose:
Characteristically for this type of cheese, the nose is not very evident, although light cream and farmhouse odours can be detected. There are also honeyed tones.

Taste:
This cheese is very mild, yet has a full creamy flavour with fruity tones.

Overall opinion of cheese:
This cheese is an ideal inclusion on a cheese board, and would complement more strongly flavoured cheeses well. It may be a touch bland for some tastes, but we feel it would be ideal for children.

Production: Judy Bell has been making Wensleydale for over ten years and production takes just over four hours. Shepherd's Purse uses pure ewe's milk and vegetarian rennet. The fresh cheeses are turned daily for ten days to ripen and ensure an even distribution of moisture. This gives Wensleydale its unique texture. It is commonly moulded into large waxed and muslin bound truckles, although baby truckles and wheels are also available.

Eating and drink: We believe that a good Wensleydale makes an ideal accompaniment to most fruits, and some desserts, particularly apple pie. It is also good with fruitcake. Ideal wine combinations would include crisp, dry whites, Chardonnay or Frascati.

Storage: Wensleydale will definitely benefit from fridge storage, and can be eaten chilled, although room temperature is preferred.

Produced: Wensleydale, Yorkshire.

Stockists: Shepherd's Purse Cheeses Ltd, Leachfield Grange Newsham, Thirsk, North Yorkshire YO7 4DJ (01845 587220).

The area of Wensleydale where the animal's graze is designated a site of Environmental Sensitivity, so the use of potentially harmful chemicals is restricted.

Wigmore

Wigmore is an English cheese that comes from the Berkshire region and was created by Anne Wigmore. It is a vegetarian cheese made from ewe's milk and is classified as a semi-soft cheese. Wigmore often wins gold medals at the British Cheese Awards. It is one of only a handful of soft ewe's milk cheeses made in Britain.

Appearance:
This cheese has a wrinkled grey rind. Wigmore is fairly firm when young but flows slightly when older (the Wigmore's mature it for two to three months). A pale yellow interior with a chalky white centre. The rind looks like it has been dusted in icing sugar.

Nose:
A very fresh aroma with a nutty tang. When cut it has a floral aroma.

Taste:
A fantastic taste, combining flavours of burnt caramel, macadamia nuts and roast lamb. The rind hides a creamy, voluptuous, sweet interior. The taste is unmistakably ewe's milk, but with a delicate fresh flavour.

Overall opinion of cheese:
Although creamy, the texture has the lightness characteristic of soft sheep's cheeses. The balance of flavours changes according to season but includes grass, herbs, and flowers. The overall impression is subtle, cool, and refreshing: the cheese does not clamour for attention, but once tried becomes compulsive. Highly enjoyable and leaves us in no doubt as to why it has won so many awards. Excellent.

Production: The curd is washed to remove excess whey, then packed in moulds to drain. The milk for the sheep's cheeses comes from four farms. Traditionally ewe's milk cheese is hard, but the Wigmore's wanted to try something different and therefore produced a creamy, soft cheese with a naturally soft rind.

Eating and drink: Made in the southeast of England by Anne Wigmore, it is not inappropriate when offered with the mild and crunchy Kentish cob nuts whose season is so short. Recommended wines include a dry Chenin Blanc from the Wetzel Family Estate, Alexander 1998 and the Quinta de la Rosa from Douro, also a white wine.

Storage: There are no special instructions in how to store this cheese. Keep it in the fridge in the paper in which you purchased it. Allow the cheese to get to room temperature before consumption.

Produced: Wigmore takes its name from its makers Anne and Andy Wigmore. They also produce the favourites Spenwood and Waterloo.

Stockists: Anne and Andy Wigmore, The Cottage, Basingstoke Road, Riseley, Reading, Berkshire, RG7 1QD (01189 884564).

Recommended:
Spenwood: A hard sheep's cheese; unpasteurised milk; vegetarian rennet. When matured for six months, Spenwood is relatively moist and mild, with a delicate but distinctive grassy tang. As is characteristic of all the Wigmore's cheeses, the flavour is precisely balanced between salty and sharp. At this age, it is ripe for the table: at eight to ten months, it becomes harder, drier, and stronger, not unlike a soft-tasting Pecorino, and is ideal for sprinkling over risotto or pasta.

Anne Wigmore began acquiring a fascination for cheese during her time studying microbiology at university. And it wasn't long before Andy, her husband, left his job as a journalist to join her.

Yorkshire Blue

Yorkshire Blue cheese is an excellent example of a traditional British blue. It is made using methods dating back nearly 1000 years! What we know today as Yorkshire Blue is actually traditional Wensleydale, a blue ewe's milk cheese, and it has been faithfully recreated by Judy Bell, of Shepherd's Purse. After experience of producing quality ewe's milk cheeses, Judy was persuaded to try her hand at a traditional blue cheese by Les Lambert, one of the premier cheesemakers in Yorkshire. Together, they embarked on the production of what was to become one of England's finest cheeses. Over a year later, in July 1990, the duo managed to successfully blue their first batch of cheese. Les died tragically shortly after this, and Judy was made all the more determined to ensure the success of their last project. Her perseverance has been rewarded, with demand for Yorkshire blue today far outweighing supply. Judy won a British Cheese Awards Gold medal for Yorkshire Blue in 1997.

Appearance:
Yorkshire Blue is characterised by a hard, greyish rind. The paste is firmer than Stilton with a light blue veined mould.

Nose:
Soft and Creamy, with a strong fungal rind, the blue is evident, yet complementary, producing a wonderfully appetising nose.

Taste:
Creamy, sweet and moist, this cheese melts in the mouth and provides a delicate yet robust alternative to Stilton.

Overall opinion of cheese:
We feel that Yorkshire Blue performs two key functions in the world of cheesemaking. It provides an ideal introduction to the joys of Blue cheese, and is a wonderful alternative to the sometimes overpowering strength of Stilton.

Production: The milk used in the production of Yorkshire blue comes from three flocks, found local to the dairy. After testing, each herd's milk is made separately into cheeses. The milk is pasteurised, and then inoculated with a starter culture, which starts the souring process. The acidity of the milk is measured until it becomes suitable for the addition of vegetarian rennet and Penicillium Roquefortii, the mould-producing enzyme. The curds are then left for the acidity in the mixture to again reach desired levels, before the whey is removed. The cheese is then broken up, salted and piled into cylindrical moulds. The moulds are left to drain overnight, before the cheeses are wrapped in muslin. The rind develops over the next 48 hours, and the cheese is then matured for ten days with regular spiking, and then for a further 12 weeks to produce the mottled moulding.

Eating and drink: Yorkshire Blue provides an excellent alternative to conventional blues on the cheese board. When eating alone, we would recommend a fairly full bodied red wine such as a Tempranillo, or even a nice dessert wine, maybe a quality Sancerre.

Storage: Room temperature is a must for enjoying this cheese, and although the rind provides protection when uncut, loose wrapping should be employed to prevent drying.

Produced: Yorkshire Blue is produced on the North York moors, and the Vale of York.

Stockists: Shepherd's Purse Cheeses Ltd, Leachfield Grange Newsham, Thirsk, North Yorkshire YO7 4DJ (01845 587220).

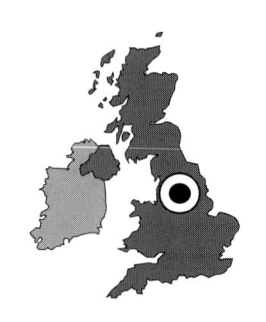

There are several versions of Yorkshire Blue available, depending on age. We recommend a fully mature cheese for a smooth creamy experience.

Basing

Type: Basing is a hard, goat's milk cheese. This is a modern, farmhouse, unpasteurised, organic cheese. It is suitable for vegetarians. The Herd contains over 300 goats with 200 milking at any specific time throughout the year. The Basing herd are one of the only commercial herds that are farmed naturally and traditionally with free range grazing. These fields are free from artificial fertilisers or weed killers. It ripens within two months and has a fat content of 45%.

Sensory Analysis: The cheese is lightly pressed, moist and crumbly. The mild and pleasant acidity, with just a hint of the herbaceous goat's milk, becomes smooth and creamier as it matures.

Produced: Maureen and Bill Browning make this cheese with milk from their own goats at Lower Basing Farm.

Stockists: Lower Basing Farm, Cowden, Kent, TN8 7JU (01342 850251).

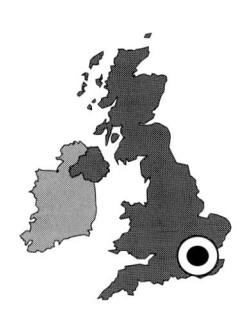

Bosworth

Type: This is a modern soft farmhouse cheese made with unpasteurised goat's milk. It is produced using a vegetarian approved rennet, and is pressed into round shapes. Affinage takes anything from three to four weeks. The cheese is sometimes known as 'Bosworth Leaf' because it is wrapped in chestnut leaves, these give a great contrast to the fluffy white bloom.

Sensory Analysis: The cheese has a surprisingly firm texture that appears breakable. The cheese melts on the palate, almost like fudge and has sweet, nutty flavours that are reminiscent of butterscotch and vanilla.

Produced: This cheese is produced by Hugh Lillington of Innes cheeses, High Field Dairy.

Stockists: Hugh Lillington, High Field Dairy, Staffordshire.

Buxton Blue

Type: This is a soft, full fat blue cheese from the Hartington Company. It is made all year round and is made from pasteurised cow's milk from cattle grazing in Derbyshire, Nottinghamshire and Staffordshire. This is a modern, creamery and vegetarian blue cheese. It ripens in ten to twelve weeks and has a fat content of around 45%.

Sensory Analysis: It usually has a cylindrical shape. Buxton Blue is mellow and russet in colour. It is normally firmer than Stilton with fine, blue streaks in the pale orange interior. This cheese has a very complex flavour with a hint of dark chocolate and a taste similar to burnt onions on the finish. When young, Buxton Blue is very mild with a hint of sharpness within a full creamy texture. The cheese has what some people describe as a honey aftertaste. It is quite crumbly and milder than most blue cheeses.
It is a table cheese used in soups, salads or simply for spreading.

Stockists: J. M. Nuttall, Hartington Creamery, Buxton.

Produced: This cheese is produced in Derbyshire at the Hartington Creamery. It is one of a few British cheeses granted the status of being a protected designation origin by the European Commission.

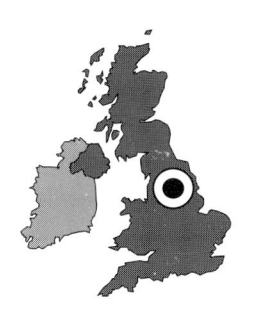

Capricorn Goats

Type: This soft, ripening goat's cheese is worthy of mention for the dimension it brings to salad alone. Made in Somerset, Capricorn Goats has won medals at the British Cheese Awards, and we feel that they are very well deserved. The cheese is available in both cylindrical or square forms and comes with a pure, white rind.

Sensory Analysis: The paste resembles a young Camembert, and can be slightly chalky when immature. The edges become creamy with age. There is a distinct nuttiness on the palate, coupled with a chicory background, which provides an ideal alternative to traditional soft, dessert cheeses. This cheese is also one of the best we sampled for grilling.

Produced: Lubborn Cheese Ltd, Somerset.

Stockists: Lubborn Cheese Ltd, Manor Farm, Cricket St. Thomas, Chard Somerset TA20 4BZ (01460 30736).

Chabis Sussex

Type: This is an unpasteurised, goat's cheese which is suitable for vegetarians. It is at its best when matured for a further couple of weeks, by which time it has opened out in flavour for a well rounded creamy floweriness and a gentle hint of goat. Kevin and Alison Blunt use a mixture of evening and morning milk from their flock, and the basic recipe they use is for a Saint-Maure, a soft creamy goat's cheese from Touraine.

Sensory Analysis: A very versatile cheese suitable for a cheese board or in the kitchen as one would use a Crottin de Chavignol. This cheese is a small, cylinder-shaped cheese with a flattened bottom. The white, bloomy rind hides a velvet texture and a medium, mellow flavour. Chabis is creamy with a fresh lemon fruitiness and a deep smoothness when it is eaten while still quite young. The unpasteurised milk gives a very creamy texture which melts in the mouth with quite a sweet finish. Smooth.

Produced: Kevin and Alison Blunt have now been making unpasteurised goat's milk cheese for over 6 years and their cheeses continue to improve, and easily compete with our continental cousins.

Stockists: K & A Blunt, Greenacres Farm, Whitesmith, Lewes, East Sussex, BN8 6JA (01825 872380).

Cooleney

Type: This is a soft Camembert style cheese produced by Breda Maher with unpasteurised cow's milk. Breda makes this cheese by hand at her farm in Tipperary, Ireland. The cheese benefits from the rich pastures where the cattle graze and that Tipperary is so famous for. When fully mature the curd is semi-liquid, this takes four to eight weeks to develop.

Sensory Analysis: This cheese is great eaten by itself, and has a soft white bloom that is mottled with brown mould. The aroma of a ripe cheese is that of mushrooms and the taste of the cheese is that of grass backed up with full, developing flavours.

Produced: This cheese is produced in Tipperary, one of the great cheeses to come out of Ireland!

Stockists: Breda Maher, Cooleeney Farmhouse Cheese, Moyne, Thurles, Co Tipperary (0504 45112).

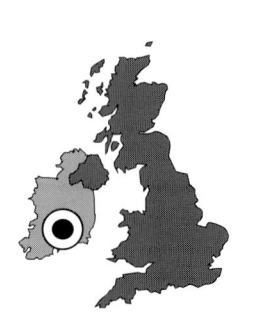

Croghan

Type: This is a semi soft goat's cheese made with vegetarian rennet. The rind is smooth, washed with brine, and terracotta in colour. Some mould may be found on the rind, but this only adds to the flavour. Made by Luc and Anne Van Kampen, the production of Croghan is loosely based on that of Gouda.

Sensory Analysis: The cheese has a very earthy flavour, with elements of both cut grass, and fresh hay, and the smooth finish is aromatic, without being overpowering. Croghan is made just from spring to autumn, and the period of affinage is around 12 weeks.

Produced: Blackwater, Co. Wexford. Ireland.

Stockists: Sheridans Cheesemongers, Kirwans Lane, Galway, Ireland (091 564 829).

Harbourne Blue

Type: This is unpasteurised, vegetarian, blue cheese of round shape made from goat's milk and one of only 3 of its kind still made in the UK. The cheese is semi-hard in style and matured for 3 months to give a very aromatic and distinctive flavour. Harbourne Blue is made by hand using only local milk, and has a fat content of 48%.

Sensory Analysis: The paste is hard and white with greeny blue mould. This cheese has a crusty natural rind. The goat's milk tends to give it a characteristically white paste and crumbly texture, and also means that it matures more quickly than a cow's milk cheese. The aroma suggests tropical fruit, and it finishes with the hot, spicy tang associated with blues. The flavour is intense but not too goaty. It is also noted that the cheese has a sweet aroma. A superb strong blue that's creamy with a good 'rustic' flavour. Recommended.

Produced: The cheese is produced by Robin Congdon and Sari Cooper of Ticklemore Cheeses in Devon.
An inspired piece of goat's milk cheesemaking from Ticklemore Cheese Company with milk from goats grazed on the edge of Dartmoor, therefore producing a very aromatic milk.

Stockists: Ticklemore Cheese Company, 1 Ticklemore, St Totnes TQ9 5EJ (01803 865926).

Leafield

Type: Leafield is a vegetarian, hard cheese made from ewe's milk. The fat content is 48% and the maturation period lasts from three to four months. In 1985, Rodney Whitworth revived the craft of making ewe's milk cheese at Abbey Farm in Goosey. Goosey means Goose Island in Old English. As well as attracting geese, the short lush grass on the island was ideal for producing ewe's milk. Rodney makes cheese in a traditional way, but he has installed modern equipment in a newly furnished dairy to ensure the highest standards of hygiene and consistency of production.

Sensory Analysis: Leafield is a hard, dense, chewy cheese, with a delightful medley of flavours. There is a certain fruitiness (rather like fresh pineapple) coupled with a nutty taste. Leafield is a wheel-shaped cheese and the rind is imprinted with a pattern that resembles the tread on a nineteenth-century steam wheel. The complex flavours are completed by a finish of hawthorn and aniseed.

Produced:. The history of Abbey Farm obviously captured Rodney Whitworth's imagination and in the late 1980's he faithfully revived the 16th century recipe for Leafield.

Stockists: Abbey Gold Cheese Farm, 6 Winters Lane, West Hanney, Oxfordshire, OX12 0LF (01235 868705).

Pentlands

Type: One of the best British Brie-like cheeses we have found. It matures to yield a rich, creamy flavour. Pentlands is only available as individual 175g cheeses. The cheese is made using pasteurised cow's milk and rennet suitable for vegetarians. It has a fat content of 48%. Pentland takes its name from the Pentland Hills which overlook the farm where the cheese was first made.

Sensory Analysis: Pentland develops a rich, soft texture and a creamy flavour and with further maturing the paste becomes runny and fuller flavoured. A mild, pasteurised soft cheese with a bloom rind and delicately flavoured. As good as Brie? We think better!

Produced: The original cheesemakers changed the name from Howgate Brie to Pentland and this lost the market for the cheese so it was taken over by Graeme Webster, with the help of Rosemary Marwick as a technical consultant. Gradually, the popularity of the cheese grew once again, but of course this time carrying the Pentland name with it.

Stockists: Howgate Farmhouse Cheesemakers, Kinfauns Home Farm Kinfauns, Perth, Perthshire PH2 7JZ (01738 443440).

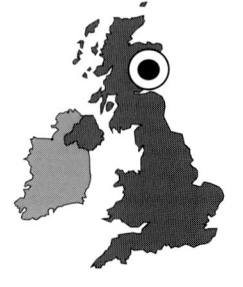

Ribblesdale

Type: Ribblesdale cheese was a bronze medal winner at the 1996 British Cheese Awards. It is made in Yorkshire and is a hard, unpasteurised farmhouse style goat's cheese. Ribblesdale is made by Iain and Christine Hill, and was created in the early eighties.

Sensory Analysis: The texture is hard and firm, similar to a young Gouda. The taste is nutty, with strong almond tones, against the familiar chicory twang of goat's cheese. Ribblesdale is coated in white wax, matures in 6 to 8 weeks, and has a fat content of around 45%.

Produced: Ribblesdale, Yorkshire.

Stockists: Ashes Farm, Horton-in-Ribblesdale, Settle BD24 0JB (01729 860231).

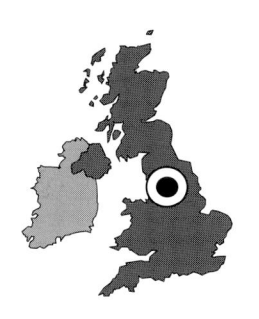

Vulscombe

Type: This beautiful cheese is produced in England by Josephine and Graham Townsend. Bizarrely, the rennet is not used to separate the milk during production – coagulation occurs solely because of the acidity of the curds.

Sensory Analysis: The finished cheese comes attractively packaged in a small, round wheel, decorated with a bay leaf, or crushed peppercorns. There is a very citrus flavour to Vulscome, but the goat's milk can also be detected. This cheese is matured for 7 to 21 days and has a fat content of around 45%.

Produced: Higher Vulscombe, Devon.

Stockists: Higher Vulscombe, Cruwys Morchard, Tiverton Devon, EX16 8NB (01884 252505).

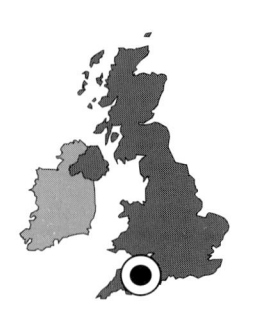

Yorkshire Feta

Type: This is a fresh cheese that originated from Greece. It grew out of a necessity for the shepherds to preserve their milk, and is one of the simplest cheeses. The cheese is often made out of the local milk type – cow's, goat's or ewe's – but ewe's is often preferred because it is very creamy and white. Once formed the cheeses are often pickled in brine for a few days and then kept in a salt solution for sale. Yorkshire Feta is not as heavily salted as some Feta's, and the cheese is waxed ready for sale. This cheese is matured for fourteen days, and the milk is provided by the ewes from the Vale of York.

Sensory Analysis: Yorkshire Feta appears very white with a crumbly texture, and has a slightly salty flavour with sweet undertones.

Produced: This cheese is produced by Shepherds Purse at the family farm near Thirsk, North Yorkshire. The company are the only producers of blue cheese in Yorkshire and have an interesting range all made with different milks.

Stockists: Shepherds Purse, Leachfield Grange, Newsham, Thirsk, North Yorkshire, YO7 4DJ (01845 587220).

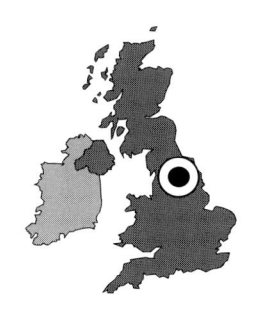

Don't Worry!
The FSA's Cheesemaking Initiative

The Food Standards Agency have recently launched a food safety management awareness initiative aimed at the producers of specialist cheeses such as classic Cheddars, traditional Stiltons and crumbly Cheshires. British consumers spend around £1.5bn generally on all types of cheese each year, and eat more than 590,000 tonnes.

There are around 450 different specialist British cheeses available today, made by 180 specialist producers. Many of these are small-scale businesses. Their products are often produced on farms from small herds or flocks using time-honoured methods involving open vats, hand-stirring, bandaging, and waxing.

The Agency, working with the Specialist Cheesemakers' Association (SCA) and other stakeholders, will promote best practice to help specialist cheesemakers continue to produce cheeses safely, and to the highest standards.

The cornerstone of the initiative is a Workbook which has been designed to reduce the burdens of food safety planning and paperwork by systematically documenting production systems and identifying food safety hazards and appropriate controls. Production systems are required to be adequately documented and recorded by law. It is important that hazards associated with specialist cheesemaking are identified and managed in a structured way throughout the stages of production.

Sir John Krebs, Chairman of the Food Standards Agency, speaking at the launch event where specialist cheeses were displayed and tasted, said:

"There has been a revolution in the British cheese industry in the last 15 years, with old recipes revived, new ones created and rare types re-established. We want to ensure that this extraordinary diversity and the superb quality of British cheeses continues to be maintained.

We know that specialist cheesemakers demonstrate time and again a real passion for their craft. The Food Safety Management system gives them a practical way in which to demonstrate excellence in standards of production and hygiene and to provide continued assurance to cheese-loving consumers. I strongly urge cheesemakers and enforcement authorities to take advantage of this opportunity to work together."

We feel that the FSA's intervention in the industry will be of great benefit in the future. The tight guidelines set down will, in our view, enable the public's confidence in British cheesemaking to rise, thus increasing sales and profits for the 180 or so independent cheesemakers around Britain.

As, during the research conducted for this book, we have begun to learn more about the world of British cheese, our views on its survival have been cemented.

As a group, we believe firmly that this initiative will help to ensure that the wonderful cheeses on offer around Britain will be going strong for years to come.

The Authors

Glossary

Acidic – This word is descriptive of a slightly sour or bitter taste when eating cheese.

Acidification – When the introduction of the starter culture causes the milk to become acidic.

Acidity – The amount of acid contained within raw milk; the milk has to reach a certain acidity before they can move onto the next stage.

Affinage – A French term describing the process of ageing and maturing of cheese.

Affineur – Somebody who takes the cheese from a cheesemaker and carries out the work of affinage, or the process of finishing off the ageing process of the cheese.

Aged – A term used to describe a cheese that has been left to mature and develop in flavour.

Annatto – This is a yellowish-red dye made from the seeds of a small tropical tree. It is used to create the orange colouring found in Red Leicester and some Cheddars.

Aroma – This is often used to describe the pleasant smell of a cheese.

Artisan – Often used to describe a skilled craftsman such as a cheesemaker, producing a traditional cheese.

Bacteria – These are tiny micro-organisms which help cheese to mature and flavour.

Bacterial Cultures – These are groups of bacteria used as starters in cheesemaking. They are used to increase the acidity of the cheese, and add flavour.

Balanced – Having the correct ratios of milk and acid in a cheese.

Barnyardy (Barny) – A description of the flavour and aroma of a cheese, it can be likened to a barnyard, strong, musty and earthy.

Bitter – A term used to describe the taste of a cheese, strong and sharp, usually unpleasant.

Bloomy rind – A soft white rind produced by spraying penicillium candidum on cheese. Examples of cheese with this type of rind include Somerset Brie and Flower Marie.

Blue-surfaced cheese – Cheeses which have blue mould on the surface of the cheese. These moulds are added both internally and externally.

Blue-veined cheese – Cheeses which have blue veins of mould running throughout the cheese. This mould is added to the curds during the production, and once formed the cheese is skewered to allow air to cause the moulds to grow.

Body – This refers to the texture of the cheese.

Brine – This is a solution made from water and salt used for preserving and enhancing the flavour of cheese. Cheese can be left in brine from a couple of hours to many months.

Brushed Rind – Natural rind cheeses are brushed to keep mould from forming on the outer surface, it also helps to keep the interior moist.

Burn – This term is used when tasting cheese to describe an intense burst of flavour which can linger. It is often used when describing Cheddar. In most circles the bigger the burn the better the cheese.

Butterfat – This describes the natural fats found within cheeses, animals have a different proportion of fat in their milk, which then affects the flavour of the cheeses.

Butterscotch – A term used to describe a caramel flavour in a cheese, usually found in aged cheeses.

Buttery – A term used to describe both the texture and the flavour of a cheese. A buttery texture has smooth milky and creamy qualities, whereas a buttery flavour is smooth, rich, and butter-like.

Casein – This is the protein found in milk which coagulates to form the curds.

Chalky – A term used to describe the pre-ripened stage of some cheeses such as Brie; the chalkiness is often found towards the centre of the cheese. It is also used to describe the undesirable texture of some goat's cheeses, soft and crumbly.

Cheddaring – A process used when making Cheddar cheese where curds are cut into small pieces in order to drain the remainder of the whey.

Clean – A term used to describe a standard cheese, which has no distinguishable flavour or lingering aftertaste.

Cloth-wrapped – Cheeses which have been wrapped or bandaged in cloth in order to be aged.

Coagulation – This is the thickening of the milk protein or casein to form the curds.

Coulommier – Used to describe Brie-like cheeses.

Cracked – A cheese having cracks on its surface; sometimes it is as a result of natural ageing, other times it is due to drying out.

Creamy – A term used to describe the texture and flavour of a cheese. A creamy cheese is smooth, fresh and usually ripe.

Crumbly – Used to describe the texture of the cheese, a crumbly texture breaks up when cut.

Curds – The solid part of the milk after coagulation.

Curing – This means the same as ripening or ageing of cheese

Dry Matter – The portion of cheese which is not liquid matter.

Earthy – A term used to describe both the taste and aroma of a cheese. It is a deep flavour and aroma having the characteristics of soil.

Explosive – A term used to describe a burst of flavour when tasting cheese, synonymous with the burn of a cheese.

Farmlike – Characteristics of a cheese similar to grass, fresh and earthy.

Fat content – Denotes the amount of fat in the dry matter of the cheese, the average is 45%, although it can be as low as 7% or as high as 75%.

Fermentation – A process in which a micro-organism breaks down the milk and turns it into cheese and other dairy products.

Firm – A term used to describe the physical characteristics of a cheese.

Fresh Cheese – These cheeses have not been aged or cured, such as cottage cheese.

Fruity – A term used to describe cheese reminiscent of fruit.

Gamy – Depending on the cheese this can be both a favourable and unfavourable term used to describe cheese with strong animal characteristics.

Grassy – A term used to describe cheese that resembles grass in its flavour and aroma, usually fresh young cheeses.

Gummy – Refers to the texture of a cheese, chewy, sticky and thick. Gumminess is usually due to excessive moisture. This is an unfavourable characteristic.

Hard – One of the main characteristics of a cheese. Hard cheeses have a low moisture content and are firm in texture. They are usually aged for many months or pressed, causing them to lose their moisture and become hard.

Herbaceous – A term associated with the flavour or aroma of a cheese. An herbaceous cheese has herbal characteristics either due to the addition of herbs, the way the cheese was made, or the type of grass or feed fed to the animal that produced the milk for the cheese.

Lactic Acid – This is the acid which is produced with the breakdown of lactose. Lactose is broken down when the starter culture is added to the milk.

Lactose – Is a naturally forming sugar present in all milk, also called milk sugar.

Mottled – This describes a cheese with different colours/shades. This can be due to the cheesemaker using milks from different vats or it may be due to the introduction of an herb, such as sage in Sage Derby.

Moulding – This is a step in the cheesemaking process where the curds are pressed into a mould. Moulds are usually plastic with perforations to allow for drainage.

Mouthfeel – This is the technical term used to describe what the cheese feels like in the mouth.

Mushroomy – The term used to describe the flavour/aroma of a cheese. This aroma can often be found on the rinds of aged cheeses.

Musty – A term used to describe cheese that smells damp and earthy, it is not a favourable characteristic.

Natural Rind – Denotes a rind which is naturally formed due to bacteria in the cheese, or bacteria that has been added to the surface. Natural rind can often be eaten, whereas unnatural rind includes wax and paraffin.

Nutty – Used to describe both the flavour and aroma of a cheese. It is a favourable flavour and is usually found on the rind of aged cheeses. The word can also imply toasty and woody flavours.

Paraffin – This is a chemical used to preserve cheese almost indefinitely.

Pasteurisation – Is the process where milk is heated to a high temperature (160°F) in order to destroy harmful bacteria. Bacteria in milk help create the flavour in the cheese, and therefore a pasteurised cheese will not have the depth in flavour as its unpasteurised equivalent.

Penicillium Candidum – This is a type of bacteria used to create bloomy rinds, such as in Somerset Brie.

Penicillium Roquefortii – A bacterial culture added to blue cheese at the start of the process to give it its blue veins.

Perfumy – A favourable term used to describe the aroma of a cheese. It is a light floral fragrant.

Pigment – This is the term used for the substance added to a cheese to give it colour. An example of a pigment would be annatto.

Piquant – A favourable term used to describe cheese having a taste, or smell that is spicy or savoury, with a subtle bitterness. This can usually be found in young goat's cheeses.

Pungent – This describes the strong musty aroma found in some aged cheeses. This aroma can be both favourable or unfavourable depending on the person. Some cheeses have a pungent aroma because they are too old or poorly made, and in this sense the attribute is undesirable.

Raw Milk – A term used to describe milk that has come directly from the animal, i.e. unpasteurised.

Rennin/Rennet – This is the enzyme used in the cheesemaking process to coagulate the milk

Rind – This is the protective outer layer of the cheese, which can either be natural or artificial.

Ripening – The process whereby cheese is stored until ripe

Runny – This term refers to the consistency of a cheese when ripe, it oozes from out of the rind; a runny cheese does not hold its form.

Rustic – These are the herbal, rustic, earthy qualities of a cheese, usually used when describing natural rind cheeses such as ewe's or goat's.

Salting – This is the part where salt is added to the cheese during the making process. Adding the salt helps extract moisture from the curds. Cheddar is made using this process.

Sharp – This term refers to the taste of a cheese and is strong, intense and slightly bitter. The sharpness of a cheese relates to the acidity of a cheese.

Silky – This is a term used to describe the texture of a cheese; a silky cheese is smooth, soft and rich.

Smoked – Cheese that has been flavoured using smoke from Cedar, Hickory or other local woods.

Smokey – This is a term used to describe a cheese that has undergone the smoking process, usually earthy and rich.

Solid – A solid cheese has no openings or cracks on its surface, and is also firm and has a strong form.

Squeakers – These refer to the balls of freshly made Cheddar scooped out and served or sold immediately. The name is meant to resemble the sound made when eating the fresh cheese curds.

Stout – This is a strong, dark beer made from roasted malted barley, which goes well with most of the farmhouse cheeses.

Surface Ripened Cheeses – Cheeses where bacteria are grown on the surface of the cheese, so that ripening starts at the surface and progresses toward the interior.

Trappist Cheese – Refers to cheese produced in the medieval monasteries of France, all having the characteristic washed rind.

Truffy – A term used to describe a cheese with earth/rustic characteristics, likened to the flavour of a truffle.

Truckle – A term used to describe the shape of a cheese – Stilton, for example.

Unpasteurised – The term used to describe a cheese which was made using unpasteurised milk. Unpasteurised milk has not been heated or treated to kill bacteria.

Washed-rind cheese – A cheese that has been usually washed in a salt solution in order to keep it moist, and add flavour. Cheeses can also be washed in beer, wine, and cider.

Wax – An unnatural coating found on some continental cheeses, such as Edam and Gouda.

Wheel – The shape that some cheeses are pressed into – Cheddar, for example.

Whey – This is the liquid which is extracted from the solid part of the milk.

Yeasty – A term used to describe the flavour or aroma of a cheese, it is reminiscent of freshly baked bread, or beer.

Useful Websites

The following websites will help you in your quest for the perfect cheese.

www.cheesemarketnews.com
www.4cheese.com
www.cheesereporter.com
www.wgx.com/cheesenet/
www.ilovecheese.com
www.cheese.com
www.teddingtoncheese.co.uk
www.igourmet.com
www.sharpham.com
www.carblife.com
www.thebigsheep.co.uk
www.cheese2u.co.uk
www.worldofcheese.com
www.legrandfromage.co.uk
www.specialtyfoods.co.uk
www.foodwales.com
www.efr.hw.ac.uk/SDA.
www.britishcheese.com/Trade/trade_f.htm.
www.camnet.uk/camra/ale/302/cheeselist.htm

www.swaledalecheese.co.uk
www.welshcheese.co.uk
www.quickes.co.uk
www.cheesemongers.co.uk
www.finecheese.co.uk
www.wensleydale.co.uk
www.cheeseandwines.co.uk
www.cheeseboard.co.uk
www.gourmetslair.co.uk
www.stilton-cheese.co.uk
www.southwest.uk.com
www.tasteofengland.co.uk
www.cheese-shop.co.uk
www.foodfirst.co.uk
www.tasteofthewest.co.uk

Acknowledgements

Many thanks to the many people who helped us not only produce this book but develop our knowledge of cheese. We would like to thank Peter Spencer for always keeping our feet on the ground and Kate Morse for her undoubted enthusaism in the world of British Cheeses. Thanks to the many suppliers for their information especially to Lisa from the Silver Hill Dairy, Ecclesall Road, Sheffield. Thanks also to the many workers in the creameries such as Debbie Mumford who allowed us to ask questions while no doubt they were supposed to be working.

Thanks also to George at Weprintbooks.com for his useful and more importantly quick responses to the many questions we had.
Thanks to Emma Smiton, who produced the artwork for the front cover.

Finally, many thanks to the team from Neals Yard Dairy who helped us develop the cheeses that we have chosen and in particular Randolph Hodgson who, despite being inundated with requests took time out to read this book and endorse it for us.

Photographs

All photographs courtesy of teddingtoncheese.co.uk except for the following:

Hereford Hop supplied by www.igourmet.com
Sharpham's supplied by www.sharphamestate.com
Red Leicester supplied by www.low-carbdiet.co.uk
Tymsboro, Durrus, Milleens are courtesy of Neal's Yard Dairy.